First Children's Encyclopedia

LONDON, NEW YORK,
MELBOURNE, MUNICH, and DELHI

Editors Penny Smith, Lorrie Mack,
Caroline Stamps, Lee Wilson
Project Art Editor Mary Sandberg
Designers Laura Roberts-Jensen, Lauren Rosier
Publishing Manager Bridget Giles
Art Director Rachael Foster
Production Editor Siu Chan
Jacket Designers Natalie Godwin,
Laura Roberts-Jensen

Contents first published in various titles of the DK First Reference series
(Illustrated Atlas, Encyclopedia, Human Body Encyclopedia, Science
Encyclopedia, Animal Encyclopedia, Nature Encyclopedia, Dinosaur
Encyclopedia, Space Encyclopedia) in Great Britain between
2002 and 2008 by Dorling Kindersley.
This edition first published in Great Britain in 2010 by
Dorling Kindersley Limited, 80 Strand, London, WC2R 0RL

2 4 6 8 10 9 7 5 3 1
176265 – 11/09

A CIP catalogue record for this book
is available from the British Library.

ISBN 978-1-40535-273-4
Colour reproduction by MDP, UK
Printed and bound by Toppan, China

Discover more at
www.dk.com

Contents

Our world

People and society

Using this book

In these pages you can find a country and discover its major features, look at culture and history, and observe wildlife and ecosystems. You can also explore the world of science – from how technology works to what's going on inside the human body. Enjoy a thrilling journey!

The **First Children's Encyclopedia** is divided into ten colour-coded chapters so you can see what you are looking for at a glance:

- Our world
- People and society
- History of people
- Human body
- The living world
- Ecosystems and habitats
- Age of the dinosaurs
- Science and technology
- Planet Earth
- The universe

What's what on a page?

The pages have special features that show you how to get your hands on as much information as possible! Look out for these:

The **Curiosity quiz** will get you searching through each section to find the pictures.

The living world

The living world

Our amazing world is filled with millions of species, or types, of living thing. They can be as big as an elephant or so small you have to look through a microscope to see them.

Spider

Animals
The animal kingdom is made up of vertebrates (animals with a backbone) and invertebrates (animals without a backbone).

Dragonfly

Micro-organisms
Micro-organisms are very tiny – they are made up of a single cell. This amoeba is magnified more than 100 times.

Mammals, birds, reptiles, amphibians, and fish are vertebrates

Coral reef

Sunflower

Deer

Snake

Insects such as butterflies are invertebrates

Plants
Plants cannot move around like animals. To survive and grow, they have to make their own food. In turn, plants provide food for many animals and fungi.

Signs of life
Living things share some characteristics. They all need food and oxygen. They also grow, reproduce, and adapt to their environment.

Fungi
Fungi (like toadstools, mushrooms, and moulds) are neither plants nor animals, but they're more like plants than animals.

Tree frog

Fungi

The living world

Curiosity quiz
Look through The living world pages and see if you can identify the pictures below.

Become an expert
126-127 Types of animals
148-149 How plants work

122

Which group of animals has the most members?

Invertebrates – they make up 97 per cent of all animal species.

123

Become an expert tells you where to look for more information on related subjects.

There is a question at the bottom of each page.

Text gives you information about a subject.

Hands on

Want to try something for yourself? Then look at a "Hands on" tip.

Hands on tells you how to get stuck in and try an experiment for yourself.

Buttons contain mini facts: quick information at your fingertips.

...of matter

...ome materials are hard and ...rittle, while others are flexible. Some materials are colourful, while others are transparent. These kinds of features are called "properties".

...is is the ...at which ...becomes a solid.

Plasticity is how well a solid can be reshaped.

Conductivity is how well a material lets electricity or heat travel through it.

Malleability is how well a solid can be shaped without breaking.

Tensile strength is how much a material can stretch without breaking.

Flammability is how easily and quickly a substance will catch fire.

Reflectivity is how well a material reflects light. Water reflects well.

Transparency is how well a material will let light pass through it.

Flexibility is how easily a material can be bent.

Solubility is how well a substance will dissolve, such as salt in water.

A cork floats on oil. Oil floats on water.

Does it float?
It's easy to learn about some properties, such as the ability to float. The amount of matter in a certain volume of an object is called its density. Objects and liquids float on liquids of a higher density and sink through liquids of a lower density.

A plastic building brick sinks through oil but floats on water.

An onion sinks through oil and water but floats on syrup. Syrup sinks below water.

A good insulator
Heat cannot easily pass through some materials. These are known as insulators. For example, aerogel can completely block the heat of a flame. But don't try this at home!

Properties of matter

Brittleness
Some materials, such as glass, are very brittle and will break when pushed out of shape. Safety glass is designed to crack rather than break.

Safety glass

Compressibility
Gases can be squashed, or compressed, by squeezing more into the same space. This is what happens when you pump up a tyre.

Gas can be compressed because its particles are far apart. A bicycle pump pushes the particles closer together.

Foot pump

Gas particles

Hardness
A scientist called Friedrich Mohs created a scale of ten minerals to compare how hard they are. Many materials are graded on this scale.

Diamond is the hardest mineral.

Corundum

Apatite

Fluorite

Feldspar

Quartz

Topaz

Gypsum

Calcite

Talc

Softest mineral

Hands on

Collect some different pebbles and put them in order of hardness. A pebble is harder than another if it scratches it. This is how Mohs worked out his scale.

A smooth flow
Some liquids flow more easily than others. It depends on their "stickiness", or viscosity. Hot lava from a volcano flows slowly because it is sticky.

224

225

Photographs show you information about a subject.

Quick quiz questions are at the bottom of each page.

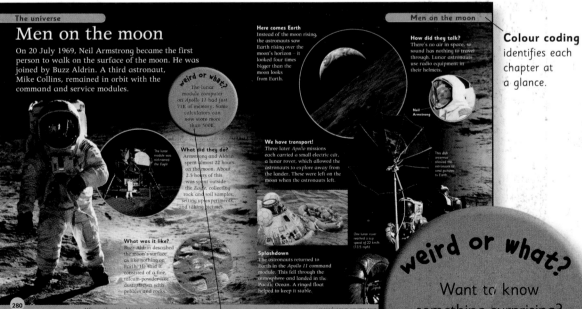

The universe

Men on the moon

On 20 July 1969, Neil Armstrong became the first person to walk on the surface of the moon. He was joined by Buzz Aldrin. A third astronaut, Mike Collins, remained in orbit with the command and service modules.

weird or what?
The lunar module computer on *Apollo 11* had just 71K of memory. Some calculators can now store more than 500K.

The lunar module was nicknamed the *Eagle*.

What did they do?
Armstrong and Aldrin spent almost 22 hours on the moon. About 2.5 hours of this was spent outside the *Eagle*, collecting rock and soil samples, setting up experiments, and taking pictures.

What was it like?
Buzz Aldrin described the moon's surface as like nothing on Earth. He said it consisted of a fine, talcum-powder-like dust, strewn with pebbles and rocks.

Here comes Earth
Instead of the moon rising, the astronauts saw Earth rising over the moon's horizon – it looked four times bigger than the moon looks from Earth.

We have transport!
Three later *Apollo* missions each carried a small electric car, a lunar rover, which allowed the astronauts to explore away from the lander. These were left on the moon when the astronauts left.

Splashdown
The astronauts returned to Earth in the *Apollo 11* command module. This fell through the atmosphere and landed in the Pacific Ocean. A ringed float helped to keep it stable.

Men on the moon

How did they talk?
There's no air in space, so sound has nothing to travel through. Lunar astronauts use radio equipment in their helmets.

Neil Armstrong

One lunar rover reached a top speed of 22 km/h (13.5 mph).

This dish antenna allowed the astronauts to send pictures to Earth.

280

Colour coding identifies each chapter at a glance.

weird or what?

Want to know something surprising? Then look at a "Weird or what?" tip.

Every page is **colour coded** to show you which chapter it's in.

Weird or what? are packed with extra weird or wonderful facts.

5

Our world

Land covers a third of planet Earth, and water and ice cover the rest. We divide the land into seven main chunks called continents. The sea is divided into five major areas called oceans.

North America

Pacific Ocean

Atlantic Ocean

Inside the Earth

The core of the Earth is made of metal – solid in the middle and molten all around it. We live on a thin, solid crust, a bit like the crust of a pie.

South America

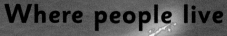

Where people live

This picture of Earth at night was taken by a satellite in space. The bright bits are made by lights on the surface. They show where the world's big cities and towns are.

How long would a trip around the Equator take at walking speed?

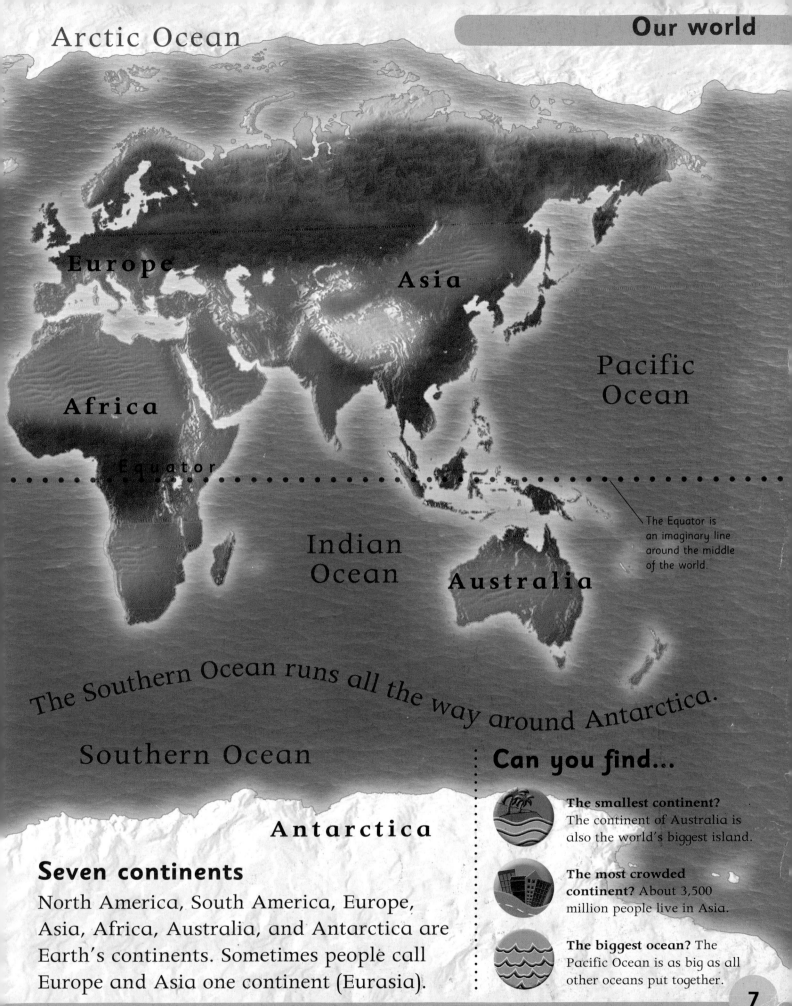

Arctic Ocean

Europe

Asia

Africa

Equator

Pacific
Ocean

The Equator is
an imaginary line
around the middle
of the world.

Indian
Ocean

Australia

The Southern Ocean runs all the way around Antarctica.

Southern Ocean

Antarctica

Can you find...

The smallest continent?
The continent of Australia is
also the world's biggest island.

**The most crowded
continent?** About 3,500
million people live in Asia.

The biggest ocean? The
Pacific Ocean is as big as all
other oceans put together.

Seven continents

North America, South America, Europe,
Asia, Africa, Australia, and Antarctica are
Earth's continents. Sometimes people call
Europe and Asia one continent (Eurasia).

About a year (without stopping for a rest).

The Arctic

At the top of the world is the North Pole, and around this is an area called the Arctic. The Arctic is mostly ocean. In its centre is a gigantic lump of floating ice that never completely melts. Further out are the northern tips of the continents and the huge island of Greenland.

Arctic people

Arctic people live in the icy lands around the Arctic Ocean. The weather is too cold for growing crops, so Arctic people get all their food from animals. They survive by fishing, herding reindeer, and hunting seals and whales.

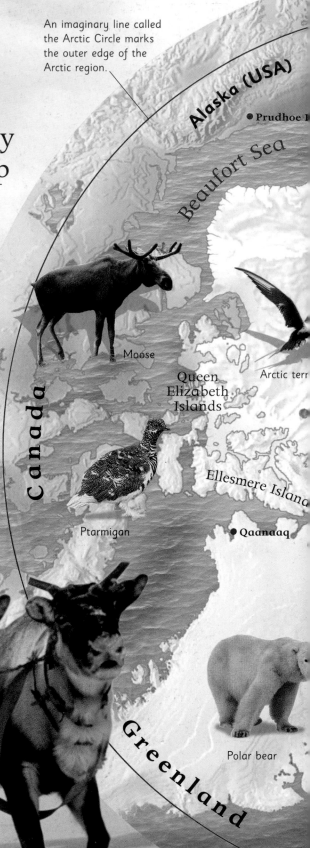

An imaginary line called the Arctic Circle marks the outer edge of the Arctic region.

Alaska (USA)

Prudhoe I

Beaufort Sea

Moose

Arctic ter

Queen Elizabeth Islands

Ellesmere Island

Canada

Ptarmigan

Qaanaaq

Polar bear

Greenland

Who was the first person to reach the North Pole?

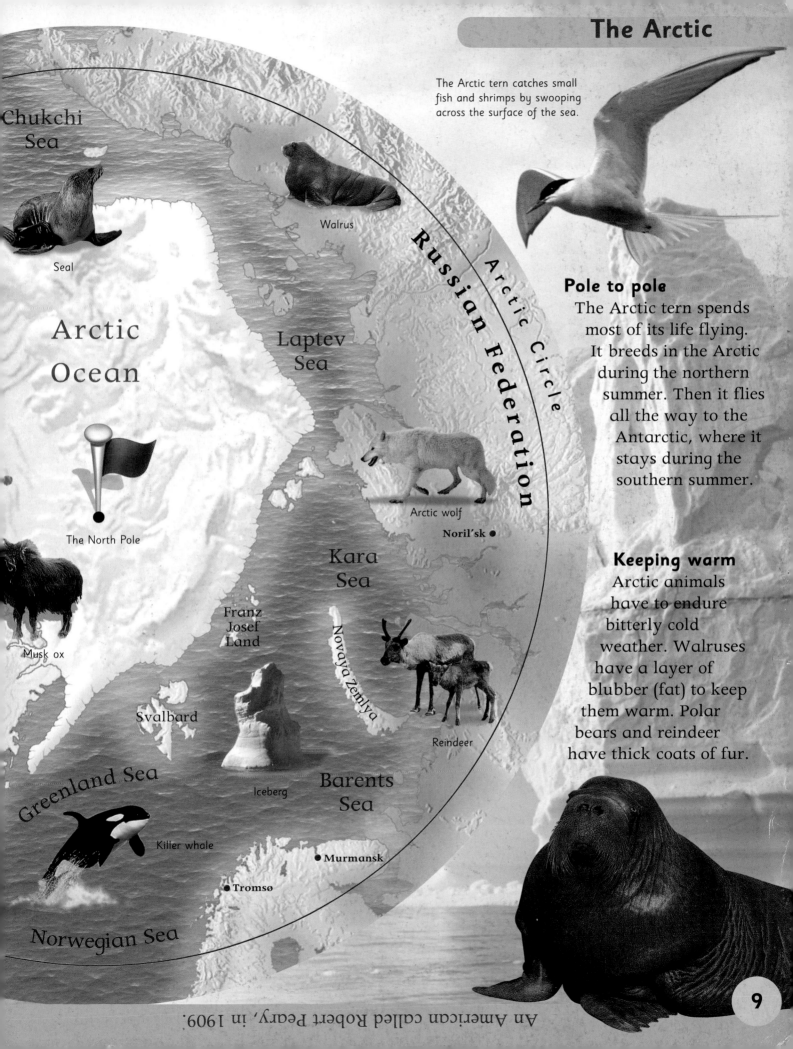

The Arctic tern catches small fish and shrimps by swooping across the surface of the sea.

Chukchi Sea

Seal

Walrus

Arctic Ocean

Laptev Sea

The North Pole

Musk ox

Arctic wolf

Noril'sk ●

Kara Sea

Franz Josef Land

Novaya Zemlya

Svalbard

Reindeer

Iceberg

Greenland Sea

Barents Sea

Killer whale

● Murmansk

● Tromsø

Norwegian Sea

Russian Federation

Arctic Circle

Pole to pole

The Arctic tern spends most of its life flying. It breeds in the Arctic during the northern summer. Then it flies all the way to the Antarctic, where it stays during the southern summer.

Keeping warm

Arctic animals have to endure bitterly cold weather. Walruses have a layer of blubber (fat) to keep them warm. Polar bears and reindeer have thick coats of fur.

9

An American called Robert Peary, in 1909.

Canada and Alaska

Canada is the second-largest country in the world, and Alaska is the largest of all the US states. Despite their huge size, both places have small populations because much of the land is covered in thick forest or frozen for most of the year.

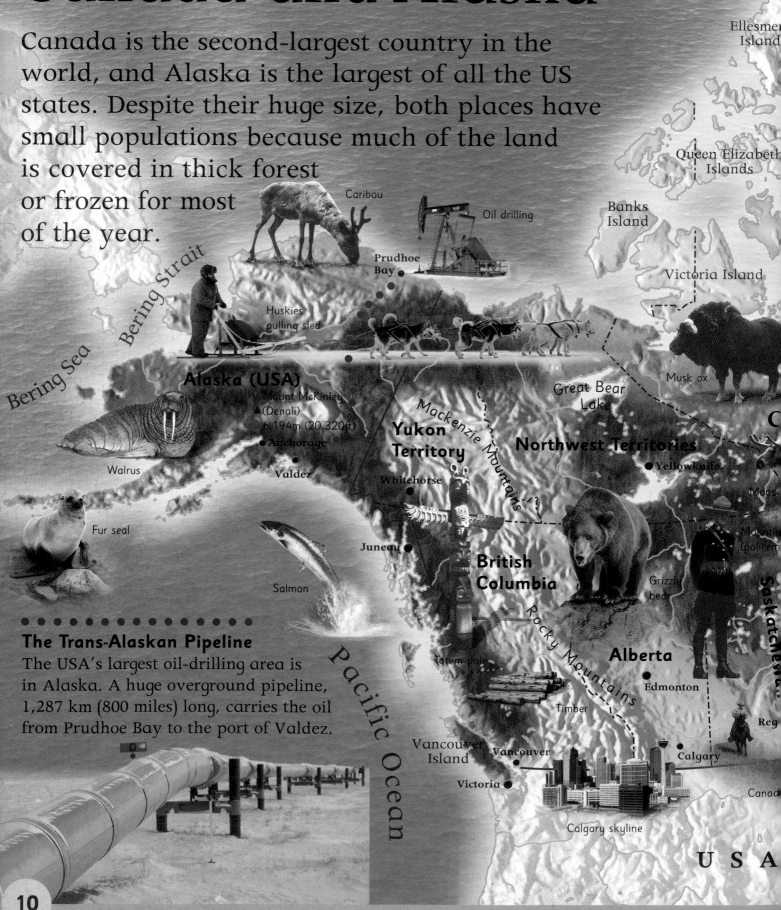

Caribou

Oil drilling

Ellesmere Island

Queen Elizabeth Islands

Banks Island

Victoria Island

Prudhoe Bay

Huskies pulling sled

Bering Strait

Bering Sea

Alaska (USA)

Mount McKinley (Denali) 6,194m (20,320ft)

Anchorage

Walrus

Valdez

Great Bear Lake

Musk ox

Mackenzie Mountains

Yukon Territory

Northwest Territories

Yellowknife

Whitehorse

Moose

Fur seal

Juneau

British Columbia

Grizzly bear

Mountie (policeman)

Saskatchewan

Salmon

Rocky Mountains

Alberta

Edmonton

Timber

Totem pole

The Trans-Alaskan Pipeline
The USA's largest oil-drilling area is in Alaska. A huge overground pipeline, 1,287 km (800 miles) long, carries the oil from Prudhoe Bay to the port of Valdez.

Pacific Ocean

Vancouver Island

Vancouver

Calgary

Victoria

Canada

Calgary skyline

U S A

What is the tallest mountain in North America, at 6,194 m (20,320 ft) high?

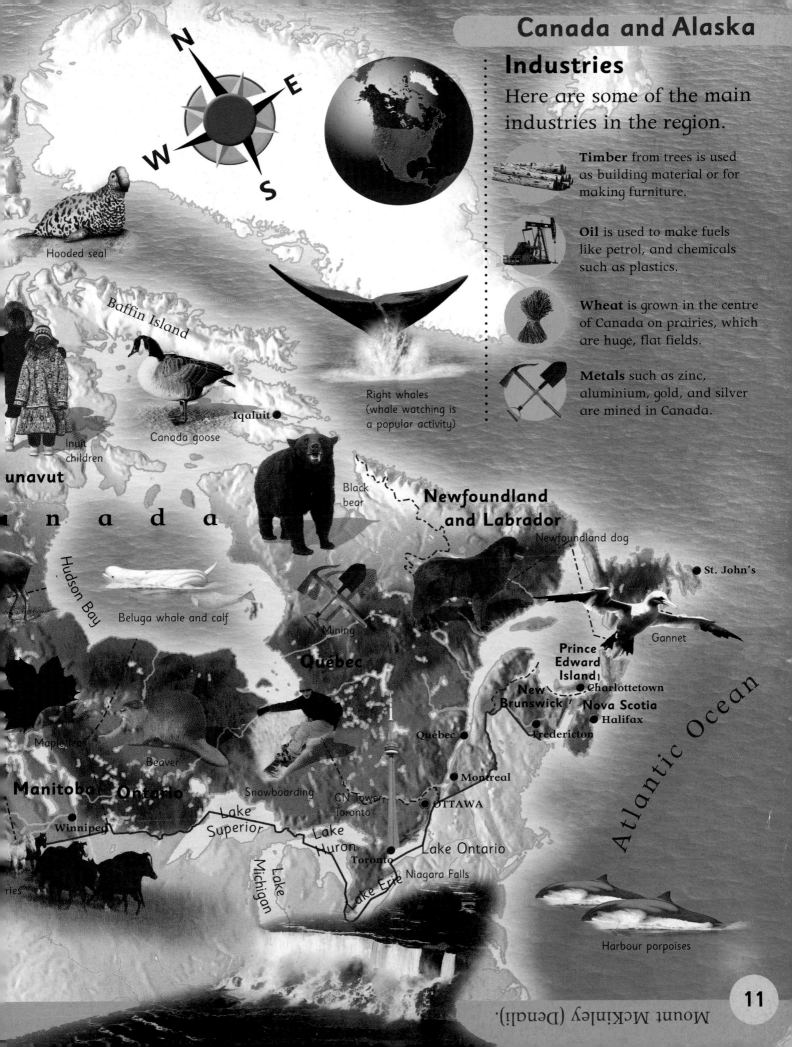

Industries

Here are some of the main industries in the region.

Timber from trees is used as building material or for making furniture.

Oil is used to make fuels like petrol, and chemicals such as plastics.

Wheat is grown in the centre of Canada on prairies, which are huge, flat fields.

Metals such as zinc, aluminium, gold, and silver are mined in Canada.

N
E
W
S

Hooded seal

Baffin Island

Inuit children

unavut

Canada goose

Iqaluit

Right whales
(whale watching is a popular activity)

Black bear

Newfoundland and Labrador

Newfoundland dog

St. John's

anada

Hudson Bay

Beluga whale and calf

Mining

Gannet

Prince Edward Island

Québec

Charlottetown

New Brunswick

Nova Scotia

Halifax

Québec

Fredericton

Maple leaf

Beaver

Montreal

Manitoba   **Ontario**

Snowboarding

CN Tower
Toronto

OTTAWA

Winnipeg

Lake Superior

Lake Huron

Lake Ontario

Toronto

Lake Michigan

Niagara Falls

ries

Lake Erie

Atlantic Ocean

Harbour porpoises

Mount McKinley (Denali).

United States of America

The United States of America is an enormous country made up of 50 states. There are mountains, deserts, forests, wetlands, and vast plains in the USA.

Technology industry

Seattle

Olympia

Washington

Columbia River

Salem

Oregon

Grizzly bear (brown bear)

Helena

Montana

Bison   Misso

Mount Rushmore National Memoria

Boise

Idaho

Skiing in the Rockies

Rocky

Mountains

Wyoming

Great Salt Lake

Golden Gate Bridge

Carson City

Mountain lion

Salt Lake City

Cheyenne

San Francisco

California

Nevada

Utah

Wheat harvest

Denver

Colorado

Pacific Ocean

HOLLYWOOD

Hollywood Hills

Los Angeles

Death Valley National Monument

Monument Valley

Colorado River

Arizona

Sonoran

Desert

Phoenix

Santa Fe

New Mexico

Roa runn

Socorro space telescope

Gila monster

Hawaii

One of the USA's 50 states is a group of eight volcanic islands in the Pacific Ocean. This state is called Hawaii.

Kauai

Niihau

Oahu   Honolulu

Molokai

Lanai   Maui

Hawaii

Mount Kilauea, on the main island of Hawaii, is the world's most active volcano.

Rio Grande

N

W   **E**

S

M e x i c o

Which is the only US state not shown on this map?

United States of America

This map shows 48 of the 50 states of the USA. The other two states are thousands of kilometres away. Alaska is northwest of Canada, and Hawaii is in the middle of the Pacific Ocean.

Canada

Lake Superior
Lake Michigan
Lake Huron
Lake Ontario
Lake Erie

Bismarck
North Dakota
Minnesota
Wisconsin
Dairy farming
Pierre
South Dakota
Iowa
Nebraska
Lincoln
Raccoon
Chicago
Sears Tower, Chicago
Illinois
Indiana
St. Louis
Topeka
Missouri
American bald eagle
Kansas
Plains
Oklahoma City
"Tornado Alley"
Oklahoma
Little Rock
Arkansas
Dallas
Texas
Oil wells
Cowboy
Baton Rouge
New Orleans
Jazz music
Louisiana
Paddle steamer
Mississippi River
Mississippi
Alabama
Montgomery
Gulf of Mexico

Michigan
Detroit
Ohio
American football
Kentucky
Ohio River
Tennessee
Country music
Atlanta
Georgia
Tallahassee
Florida
The Everglades
American alligator
Miami

New York
Maine
Augusta
Blueberries
Vermont
New Hampshire
Boston
Massachusetts
Rhode Island
Connecticut
Statue of Liberty
New York
New Jersey
Pennsylvania
Harrisburg
Delaware
Maryland
WASHINGTON DC
West Virginia
The Capitol building, Washington, DC
Virginia
Raleigh
North Carolina
South Carolina
Appalachian Mountains
Kennedy Space Center
Dolphin-watching

Atlantic Ocean

13

Alaska (see page 10-11).

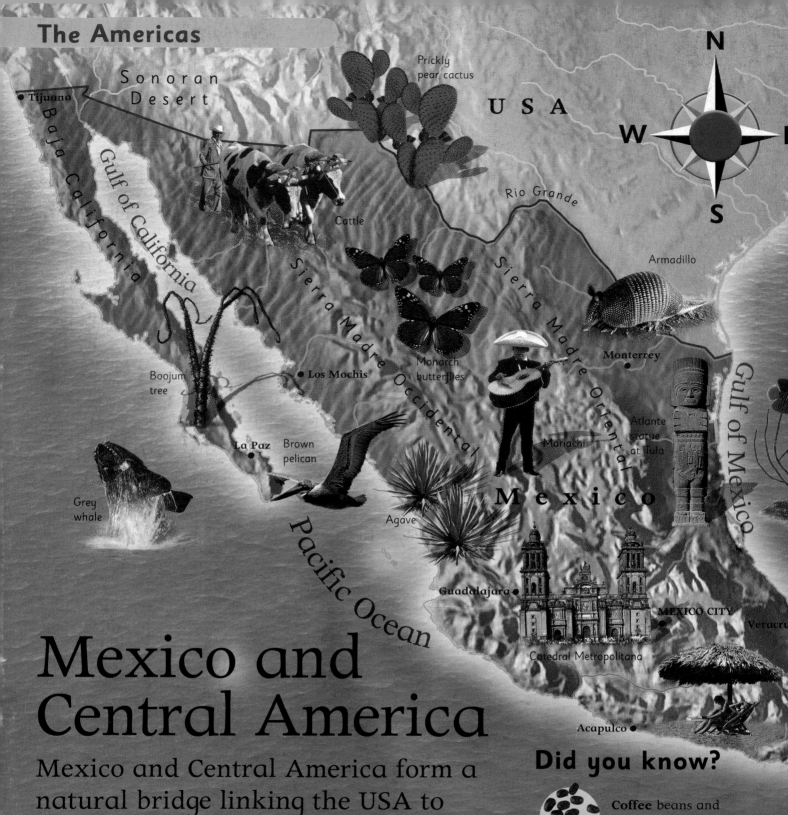

Sonoran Desert

Prickly pear cactus

USA

Tijuana

Rio Grande

Baja California

Gulf of California

Cattle

Armadillo

Sierra Madre Occidental

Sierra Madre Oriental

Monarch butterflies

Monterrey

Gulf of Mexico

Boojum tree

Los Mochis

La Paz

Brown pelican

Mariachi

Atlante statue at Tula

Mexico

Grey whale

Agave

Guadalajara

MEXICO CITY

Veracruz

Pacific Ocean

Catedral Metropolitana

Acapulco

Mexico and Central America

Mexico and Central America form a
natural bridge linking the USA to
South America. The north of Mexico
is dry and dusty. As you travel south,
the weather gets rainier and the land
becomes greener, with lush rainforests
covering mountains and volcanoes.

Did you know?

Coffee beans and
bananas are Costa Rica's
most important crops.

Chocolate was first
made in Mexico, from the
seeds of the cacao tree.

Sugar cane from Central
America and the Caribbean
is used to make sugar.

14

How do spider monkeys use their tails?

West Indies

To the east of Central America is a chain of tropical islands called the West Indies. The weather here is warm all year, but hurricanes can strike in summer.

Bahamas
NASSAU

HAVANA
Cuba

Palm tree

Pineapples

Atlantic Ocean

Greater Antilles

Haiti
PORT-AU-PRINCE

Dominican Republic

SANTO DOMINGO

SAN JUAN
Puerto Rico (USA)

Lesser Antilles

Jamaica
KINGSTON

Dominica

St Lucia

Caribbean Sea

Yacht

Barbados

PORT-OF-SPAIN
Trinidad and Tobago

Frigate

Flamingos

Chichén Itzá

Coral reef

Olmec head

Macaw

Belize
BELMOPAN

Green turtle

Grapefruit

Panama Canal

The man-made Panama Canal links the Atlantic and Pacific Oceans. About 12,000 ships pass through it every year, making it one of the world's busiest waterways.

Shrimp

Guatemala **Honduras**

TEGUCIGALPA

GUATEMALA CITY

El Salvador
SAN SALVADOR

Bananas

Nicaragua
MANAGUA Lake Nicaragua

Spider monkey

Panama Canal

Costa Rica
SAN JOSÉ **Panama**

PANAMA CITY

Toucan

Hands on

Cut the leafy top off a pineapple and plant it in a pot of soil. If you keep it in a greenhouse, it will grow into a pineapple plant.

As hooks to hang from branches.

South America

A vast chain of mountains runs the length of this continent. On its western side is the world's driest desert. On the east is the biggest rainforest.

Equator walkabout

The Equator is an imaginary line around the Earth's middle. It would take you a month to walk across just the South American part of it!

CARACAS

Venezuela

GEORGETOWN

PARAMARIBO

CAYENNE

French Guiana (France)

Guyana

Suriname

Orinoco River

Angel Falls

Agrias butterfly

Cartagena

BOGOTA

Colombia

QUITO

Ecuador

Equator

Amazon Rainforest

Belém

Capuchin

Brazil

Brazil nuts

Bananas

Manaus

River Amazon

Jaguar

Jaguar

Condor

Andes Mountains

Peru

Machu Picchu

LIMA

Arequipa

Titicaca

Lake

LA PAZ

Bolivia

Pacific Ocean

What is the highest mountain in the Andes?

Oil rig

football

●BRASILIA

Sugar Loaf Mountain

São Paulo ● Rio de Janeiro

Atlantic Ocean

N E S W

Green turtle

Can you find...

The world's highest capital?
La Paz, Bolivia, is 3,632 m (11,916 ft) above sea level.

The world's highest waterfall?
Angel Falls in Venezuela measures 979 m (3,212 ft) from top to bottom.

The world's driest town?
Arica in Chile's Atacama Desert has an annual rainfall of zero!

Gaucho

Bolivian Indian

Paraguay

●ASUNCION

Argentina

Pampas grass

Uruguay

BUENOS ● MONTEVIDEO
AIRES

● Bahia Blanca

P a m p a s

Cape Horn

The southern tip of South America is called Cape Horn. The seas around it are so stormy that hundreds of ships have been shipwrecked there.

Andes Mountains

Chile

Atacama Desert

Aconcagua

Valparaiso ● ● SANTIAGO

Sheep farming

Magellan penguins

P a t a g o n i a

Cape Horn

Mackerel

Aconcagua, which is 6,960 m (22,834 ft) high.

Africa

Africa is a vast, sun-baked continent, famous for its amazing wildlife. In the north and south are hot deserts. Between the deserts are swampy rainforests and grasslands full of wild animals.

N E W S

Asia

Red Sea

Mediterranean Sea

Suez Canal

CAIRO

River Nile

Aswan

Pyramids

Egypt

Nile felucca boat

Nubian Desert

KHARTOUM

Sudan

Eritrea

ASMERA

Great Rift Valley

Djibouti

Horn of Africa

ADDIS ABABA

Ethiopia

Gulf of Sirte

TRIPOLI

Al 'Aziziyah

Libya

Bedouin weaver

Cheetah

Chad

Lake Chad

NDJAMENA

hippopotamus

Central African Rep.

TUNIS

Tunisia

ALGIERS

Algeria

Erg Tifernine

Ahaggar Mountains

Sahara Desert

Niger

Ostriches

Sahel

NIAMEY

Cameroon

Ait Benhaddou mud fortress, Morocco

Atlas Mountains

Morocco

RABAT

Tuareg nomads

Mali

River Niger

Nigeria

ABUJA

Benin

Togo

Ghana

Cocoa bean

LAAYOUNE

Western Sahara

Mauritania

NOUAKCHOTT

Peanuts

Senegal

DAKAR

Gambia

Guinea-Bissau

Guinea

Bambara village

Burkina

Sierra Leone

Ivory Coast

Liberia

Atlantic Ocean

How long is Africa from north to south?

Can you find...

The highest point in Africa?
Mount Kilimanjaro in Tanzania is 5,895 m (19,341 ft) tall.

One of the world's highest sand dunes? Erg Tifernine in the Sahara is 400 m (1,300 ft) tall.

The hottest place on Earth?
Al 'Aziziyah, in Libya, has had temperatures of 58°C (136.4°F).

The Suez Canal
This canal is a man-made waterway that runs from the Red Sea to the Mediterranean. It provides a short cut for ships travelling from Europe to Asia.

Savanna wildlife
Much of Africa is covered by a type of grassland called savanna. Huge herds of grazing animals live on the savanna, as well as lions, hyenas, and cheetahs.

Madagascar
The island of Madagascar is home to tree-dwelling animals called lemurs. They have faces like cats but bodies like monkeys.

Atlantic Ocean

Mozambique Channel

Madagascar

ANTANANARIVO

Lemur

Chameleon

Dhow sailing boat

Mount Kilimanjaro
5,895 m (19,341 ft)

Kenya
NAIROBI

Serengeti

Lake Victoria
KAMPALA

Rwanda

Burundi

DODOMA

Tanzania

Malawi

Great Rift Valley

Masai herder

Elephant

Dem. Rep. of Congo

Zebra

Zambia

LUSAKA

Zambezi River

Angola

HARARE

Zimbabwe

Victoria Falls

Botswana

Kalahari Desert

PRETORIA

MAPUTO
Swaziland

Mozambique

Lesotho

Ndebele house

South Africa

Cape Town

Cape of Good Hope

Springbok

Tin and copper mining

Namibia

WINDHOEK

Namib Desert

Giraffe

Hornbill

LUANDA

Oil rig

Gabon

Congo

Scandinavia

The northernmost part of Europe is Scandinavia – a region of dense pine forests, snowy mountains, and craggy coastlines.

Iceland

Iceland is a volcanic island in the far north Atlantic Ocean. It has hundreds of hot springs and geysers.

Church of Hallngrímur

REYKJAVÍK

Greenland Sea

Vatnajökull (Ice sheet)

Geyser

Russian Federation

Arctic Ocean

North Cape

Lapland

Sweden

Gulf of Bothnia

Reindeer

Wolf

River Kemijoki

Oulu

Sauna

Paper mill

Grey seal

Kjølen Mountains

Wolverine

Norwegian Sea

Atlantic Ocean

Fishing trawler

Tromsø

Mining

Vest Fjord

Puffin

Which Scandinavian warriors raided Europe in 800–1050 CE?

The Øresund Bridge

The Øresund Bridge links Copenhagen in Denmark to Malmö in Sweden. There are three parts to the bridge — an underground tunnel, an artificial island, and a bridge over the sea. Together, they are 16 km (10 miles) long.

Faeroe Islands

These islands are part of Denmark. They lie halfway between Iceland and Scotland.

Torshavn

Finland

Rainbow trout

Cathedral, Helsinki

HELSINKI

Gulf of Finland

Åland Islands

STOCKHOLM

Rune stone

Gotland

Öland

Baltic Sea

Bornholm

N W E S

Golden eagle

City Hall, Stockholm

Cross-country skiing

Lake Vänern

Lake Vättern

Swedish glass

Gothenburg

COPENHAGEN

Malmö

Little Mermaid statue, Copenhagen

Norway

Stave church

▲ Mount Galdhøpiggen 2,469 m (8,100 ft)

OSLO

Sculptures in Vigeland Park, Oslo

Oslo Fjord

Nord Fjord

Sogne Fjord

Hardanger Fjord

Bokna Fjord

Bergen

Stavanger

Denmark

Dairy farming

Pig farming

Lego

North Sea

Herring

The Vikings.

21

UK and Ireland

The United Kingdom is made up of England, Scotland, Wales, and Northern Ireland. Ireland is a separate country. Most of the people in the UK and Ireland speak English as their main language.

The Royal Family

England and Scotland had separate royal families until 1603, when they joined together to form the United Kingdom. Queen Elizabeth II is the current Head of State.

North Sea

Shetland Islands

Orkney Islands

Thurso

Red deer

Outer Hebrides

Skye

Mull

Highland cow

Ben Nevis
1,343 m (4,406 ft)

Grampian Mountains

Loch Ness Monster

Aberdeen

Scotland

Bagpiper

Edinburgh

River Forth

Glasgow

Edinburgh Castle

Giant's Causeway

Angel of the North

Newcastle upon Tyne

Northern Ireland

What is the name of the Queen's official residence in London?

North Sea oil rig

Yacht

Norfolk Broads

Cambridge

Big Ben

Dover

Kingston upon Hull

Middlesbrough

Eurotunnel to France

England

LONDON

Royal Pavilion

Brighton

Oxford

River Thames

Lake District

Pennines

Blackpool Tower

Manchester

Football

Birmingham

Crufts dog show

River Severn

Isle of Wight

Liverpool

Snowdonia

Cambrian Mountains

Wales

Cardiff

Stonehenge

English Channel

Douglas

Isle of Man

Irish Sea

Portland Bill lighthouse

F r a n c e

E x m o o r

Sheep

Exeter

D a r t m o o r

Eden Project

Guinness

DUBLIN

Ireland

Galway

Blarney Castle

Cork

Jaunting car

Surfing

Land's End

Isles of Scilly

Cathedral

N E S W

The Eden Project, Cornwall
These giant greenhouses are home to lots of plants from different areas of the world. People can visit here to learn how important nature is to the future of the planet.

Buckingham Palace.

The Low Countries

Belgium, the Netherlands, and Luxembourg are called the Low Countries because they are so flat. They are also sometimes called Benelux – the first letters of BElgium, NEtherlands and LUXembourg.

Netherlands

Germany

Avocet

West Frisian Islands

Waddenzee

Ice skating

Cattle

Cyclist

Horses

IJsselmeer

Flevoland

Windmills

River Rhine

Arnhem

Tern

Cheese porters

Tulips

AMSTERDAM

Rotterdam

Barge

Antwerp Cathedral

North Sea

THE HAGUE

Cubic Houses

Fishing

Herring

Dams to stop floods from sea

Bruges Town Hall

Bruges

Ostend

N
E
S
W

24

Did you know..?

Brussels is the capital of Europe. It is the centre of the European Union and home of the European Parliament.

900 windmills along the Netherlands' coast help to keep the land drained.

Wooden clogs were first invented by Dutch workmen 600 years ago.

Belgium

The Atomium

BRUSSELS

Chocolates

Lace making

Crystal

Charleroi

River Meuse

Liege

Deer

Ardennes

Ardennes Forest

Wild boar

Beer

Vianden castle

France

Amsterdam

The tall houses lining the canals of Amsterdam were built by rich spice merchants hundreds of years ago. Each one is unique, and many are crooked because they are built on marshy land.

Luxembourg

LUXEMBOURG

Holland.

France

France is the biggest country in western Europe. Its capital is the city of Paris, site of the Eiffel Tower. France is famous for its scenic countryside, which is dotted with sleepy villages and fairytale castles called châteaux.

Mont St-Michel

A towering abbey sits on the island of Mont St-Michel off the north coast of France. At low tide, people can walk across the sand to get to Mont St-Michel.

English Channel

Mont St-Michel

Breton woman

Bayeux Tapestry

Le Mar race tra

● Rennes

Le Mans

Standing Stones (Carnac)

Mackerel

Beef cattle

Brandy

Atlantic Ocean

● Bordeaux

Bay of Biscay

Wine

Cave Paintin at Lascaux

● Biarritz

Aeroplane manufacturing

● Toulo

Pyrenees

Where in France would you find pink flamingos and wild horses?

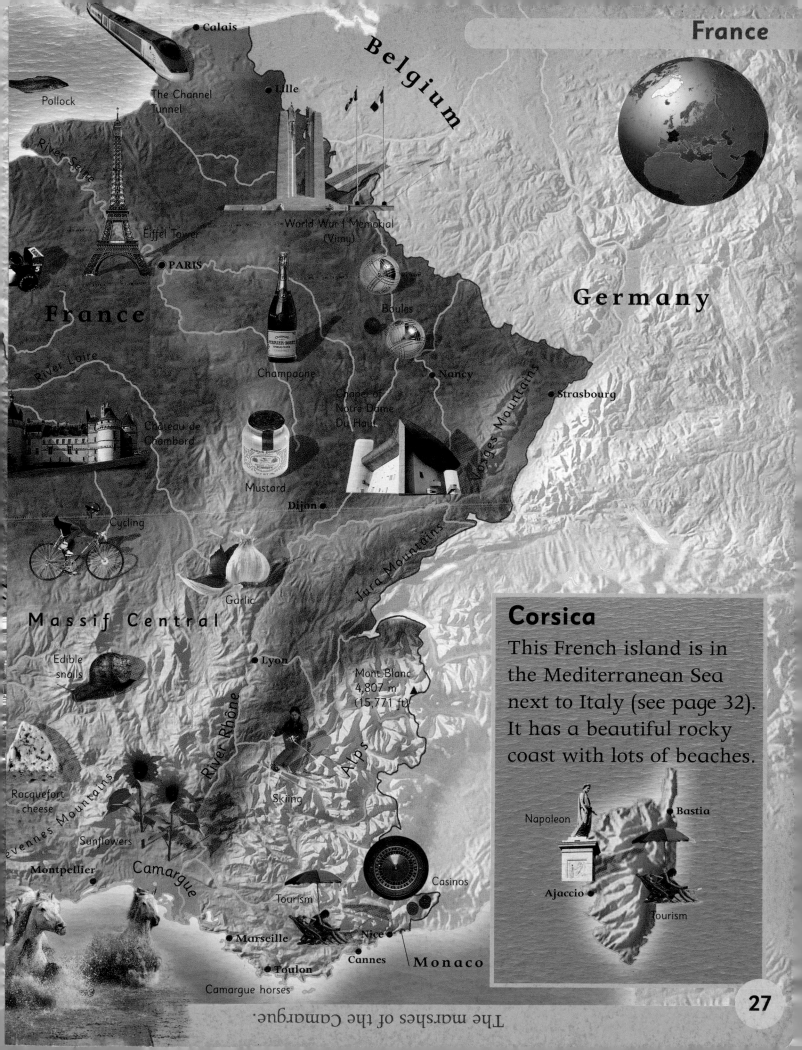

Calais

Pollock

The Channel Tunnel

Lille

Belgium

World War 1 Memorial (Vimy)

Germany

Eiffel Tower

River Seine

PARIS

France

Boules

Champagne

River Loire

Nancy

Strasbourg

Chapel of Notre Dame Du Haut

Château de Chambord

Mustard

Vosges Mountains

Dijon

Cycling

Garlic

Jura Mountains

Massif Central

Edible snails

Lyon

Mont Blanc 4,807 m (15,771 ft)

Roquefort cheese

Cévennes Mountains

River Rhône

Alps

Skiing

Sunflowers

Montpellier

Camargue

Tourism

Casinos

Marseille

Nice

Cannes

Monaco

Toulon

Camargue horses

Corsica

This French island is in the Mediterranean Sea next to Italy (see page 32). It has a beautiful rocky coast with lots of beaches.

Napoleon

Bastia

Ajaccio

Tourism

27

The marshes of the Camargue.

Spain and Portugal

Spain and Portugal are in the sunny southwest corner of Europe. Together they make up a region called the Iberian Peninsula.

Azores

Dolphin

These Portuguese islands are in the Atlantic, about a third of the way to the USA.

Ponta Delgada

Madeira

Grapes

The Portuguese island of Madeira is famous for making a rich type of wine also called Madeira.

Funchal

Canary Islands

These seven Spanish islands are off the west coast of Africa.

Lanzarote

La Palma

Santa Cruz de Tenerife

Fuerteventura

Tenerife

Gran Canaria

Banana plantations

Mountain bike

Rain

Santiago

León

Santiago Cathedral

Coal mine

Atlantic Ocean

Oporto

Salamanca

Clay cockerel (symbol of Portugal)

Portugal

Coimbra

Windmills

Riv

Belem Tower

Badajoz

LISBON

Sheep

Packing fish

Flamenco dancer

Riv

Seville

Algarve

Tourists

Lagos

Faro

Lynx

Bae

Crayfish

Wind surfing

Gibraltar (UK)

France

Andorra

Guggenheim Museum

● Bilbao

Basque Country

Mountain goat

Pyrenees

ANDORRA LA VELLA

Skiing

Wild boar

Iberian Mountains

lladolid

Spain

River Ebro

Barcelona

Marqués de Joseph

Rioja wine

Sagrada Familia Cathedral, Barcelona

N

W — E

S

Roman aqueduct

● MADRID

Sardines

Balearic Islands

Minorca

Mahón ●

gus

Majorca

● Palma

Paella

Bull-fighting

Royal Palace

Valencia

Ibiza

● Ibiza

Albacete ●

Oranges

Formentera

Mediterranean Sea

uadalquivir

Andalusian horse

● Alicante

Costa Blanca

Majorca
The Spanish island of Majorca is one of Europe's top tourist destinations. Its rugged coast has lots of picturesque beaches.

Guitar

● Cartagena

Andalusia

Olives and oil

● Granada

untains

● Malaga

Costa del Sol

Jet ski

Santiago.

Italy

Italy is shaped like a boot, with the top in the Alps mountains and the toe swimming in the Mediterranean Sea. The Apennine mountains run like a bone down the leg.

Italian lakes

There are 23 lakes in the lake district in northern Italy. Lake Garda is the biggest, and a popular place to sail and windsurf.

Skier

Dolomites

Mountain goat

Lake Garda

Milan

Wine

Turin

A l p s

Venice

Venetian gondola

River Po

Ferrari

Tagliatelli carbonara

Bologna

San Marino

Leaning Tower of Pisa

Pisa

Florence

Florence Cathedral

Moped

Fishing boat

Tuna

How many islands make up Malta?

Octopus

Crab

Wine

Taranto

Italy

Apennines

Vatican City

ROME

The Colosseum (Rome)

Pizza

Naples

Amalfi

Pompeii

Mount Vesuvius

Olives and olive oil

Cast of a body at Pompeii

Sheep

Oranges

Almonds

Squid

Messina

Noto Cathedral

Scuba diving

Syracuse

Mount Etna

Sicily

Palermo

Agrigento

Lemons

Temple of Castor and Pollux

Malta

VALLETTA

Sardinia

Sardines

Wild boar

Cagliari

Tourism

Amalfi

Mediterranean Sea

Can you find...

Europe's largest volcano?
Mount Etna in Sicily is also Europe's most active volcano.

The world's most wonky tower?
The Leaning Tower of Pisa is a campanile, or bell tower.

Where the first pizza was made? A baker in Naples invented the pizza in the 1800s.

Three: Malta, Gozo, and Comino.

Central Eastern Europe

These countries were under communist rule until the 1990s. Today they are modern nations with thriving industries. Traditional farming continues in the rural areas.

Did you know?

The Polish town of Torun is well-known for its **gingerbread**.

Budapest is split by the Danube. Buda is on one bank, Pest on the other.

The snow-white **Lipizzaner horse** is bred in Slovenia.

Baltic Sea

Canoeing

Mazury lakes

Gdansk

Koszalin

Szczecin

Ship building

Windmills

Potato farming

Mining

Torun

Poznan

Pig farms

River Oder

Wroclaw

Lodz

Gingerbread

Pig farms

WARSAW

Chemical industry

European bison

Market Square, Warsaw

River Vistula

Lublin

Sugarbeet

Skiing

Kielce

Krakow

Cattle farms

Poland

Germany

Karlovy Vary

PRAGUE

Charles Bridge

Hradec Kralove

River Elbe

Plzen

What ingredient makes Hungarian goulash spicy?

Czech Republic

Pilsner lager

Brno

Skoda

Slovakia

High Tatra Mountains

Spissky Hrad castle

Painted Easter eggs

Wooden house

BRATISLAVA

Tokay wine

Eger

Nyiregyhaza

Debrecen

Parliament, Budapest

Romania

Szeged

Horses

Goulash

BUDAPEST

Gyor

Hungary

River Danube

Pecs

Osijek

Wine

Austria

Lipizzaner mare and foal

LJUBLJANA

Slovenia

ZAGREB

Croatia

Dalmatian

Dinaric Alps

Rijeka

Tourism

Split

Dubrovnik

Adriatic Sea

High Tatra Mountains
This mountain range lies in Poland and Slovakia, and forms part of the Carpathian Mountains. The tallest peak is 2,655 m (8,710 ft) high.

N
E
S
W

Paprika

Black Sea

Southeast Europe

The mighty River Danube winds its way across southeast Europe, forming a natural border between Romania and Bulgaria. Further south are the scattered ruins of Ancient Greece.

Carpathian Mountains

Wolf

River Danube

Bran Castle, Transylvania

Varna

Burgas

Natural yoghurt

Ruse

Alexander Nevsky Cathedral

Parliament Palace

Pleven

Kazanluk

Folk dancers at Kazanluk, Festival of Roses

Roses

Sibiu

Romania

Transylvanian Alps

SOFIA

Bulgaria

Wild boar

Satu Mare

Timişoara

Goats

Grapes

BELGRADE

Macedonia

Traditional Serbian costume

Serbia

PRISTINA

SKOPJE

Kosovo (disputed)

Serbian Ražnjiči Kebab

PODGORICA

Montenegro

Oranges

Dinaric Alps

Bosnia and Herzegovina

SARAJEVO

Banja Luka

Statue in Liberation Square, Sarajevo

Mostar

Adriatic Sea

What is Greece's most important crop?

N E S W

Turkey

Rhodes

Sponge

Bouzouki

Lesbos

Chios

Dolphins

Aegean Sea

Cyclades

Knossos Palace

Iráklion

Crete

Salonica

Olive oil

Greece

●ATHENS

Ceremonial soldier from Athens

Mediterranean Sea

Bitola

Greek coffee

Pindus Mountains

Greek vase

Parthenon

Patras

Peloponnese

Greek church

Albania

Watermelon

Cephalonia

Zakinthos

Octopus

Sailing ship

Can you find…

A sponge? Old-fashioned bathroom sponges are the skeletons of dead sea creatures.

Yoghurt? People in Bulgaria eat lots of yoghurt because they think it helps them live longer.

Greek coffee? Greek people make coffee by boiling ground coffee in a tiny pan of water until it foams.

Chios Island in the Aegean Sea

Olives.

Middle East

This part of the world is hot and dry, with large deserts. Three of the world's great religions began here.

Istanbul

Blue Mosque   ANKA

Turkey

Mediterranean Sea

NICO
Cyprus

Sculpte
menora
Jerusal

Mecca

The holiest place for a Muslim is the Ka'ba, a cube-shaped shrine in Mecca. Muslims face the Ka'ba when they pray and try to visit it at least once in their lifetime.

World's first skyscrapers

The people of Yemen started building mud-brick skyscrapers thousands of years ago. The ground floors are used for animals or for storing goods. Families live in the upper floors.

Fruits of the desert

Farmers can grow crops only in the wettest parts of the Middle East.

Figs are soft, sticky fruits that can be dried to make them last longer.

Olive trees are grown for their fruit, which is pressed to make olive oil.

Dates are the fruit of palm trees, which grow by rivers and in oases.

Which country produces 65 per cent of the world's hazelnuts?

Black Sea

Whirling
Dervish dancer

Mount Ararat
5,165 m
(16,945 ft)

Head of Zeus

Caspian Sea

Syria

Olives

BEIRUT

Lebanon

Figs

DAMASCUS

BAGHDAD

AMMAN

JERUSALEM

Jordan

Iraq

TEHRAN

Turquoise

Iran

Chador, traditional
dress for women

Iranian food – chicken kebab

Marsh Arab reed house

Falconry

Ancient city
of Petra

Kuwait

KUWAIT
CITY

The Gulf

Persepolis palace

Desert
oasis

MANAMA
Bahrain

Oman

Qatar

ABU DHABI

Mecca

RIYADH

Oil

DOHA

Gulf of Oman

Red Sea

Saudi Arabia

**United
Arab Emirates**

MUSCAT

Mecca

Arabian desert

Oil refinery

Coral reefs grow
along the coast
of the Red Sea,
where the water
is warm and clear.

Oman

Camels

Desert oryx

N

Oil tanker

W   E

Yemen

S

Frankincense tree

SANA

Arabian Sea

Turkey

Southern Asia

Southern Asia is colourful and crowded. India is the biggest country in the region, with a population of more than a billion.

Elephants on parade

During the festival of Puram in southern India, 101 elephants march through the town of Trichur in a grand parade.

Snow leopard

Lapis lazuli

Decorated lorry

Afghanistan

Herat

●KABUL

Quetta

Pakistan

Tomb of Muhammad Ali Jinnah

ISLAMABAD●

Multan

Golden Temple

Delhi ●NEW DELHI

Agra

Taj Mahal

Dancer

Hyderabad ●

India

Rickshaw

Camel market

Karachi ●

Green turtles

River Ganges

River dolphin

Sacred cow

Tea picking

Imphal

Bangladesh

DHAKA

Kolkata

Rickshaw

River Narmada

When Hindus die, where are their ashes scattered?

Bay of Bengal

Arabian Sea

Coconut tree and coconut

Andaman Islands (India)

Nicobar Islands (India)

Fishing boat

N E S W

Cuttack

Common lobster

Mullet

Thresher shark

Tiger

Vijayawada

Chennai (Madras)

Jaffna

Sri Lanka

Kandy

Tea leaves

COLOMBO

Snake charmer

Mumbai (Bombay)

Indian elephant

Calicut

Kathkali Dancer

Trichur

Tuna fish

The Monsoon

Southern Asia is normally hot and dry, but every summer it pours down for weeks. This rainy season, called the monsoon, helps farmers grow crops like rice.

Can you find...

Lapis lazuli? This precious stone was once used to make brilliant, sky-blue paint.

An Indian dancer? Classical dancers use movements of their bodies to tell ancient stories.

Ganges river dolphin? This dolphin is almost blind and finds its way in muddy water by sound.

In the River Ganges.

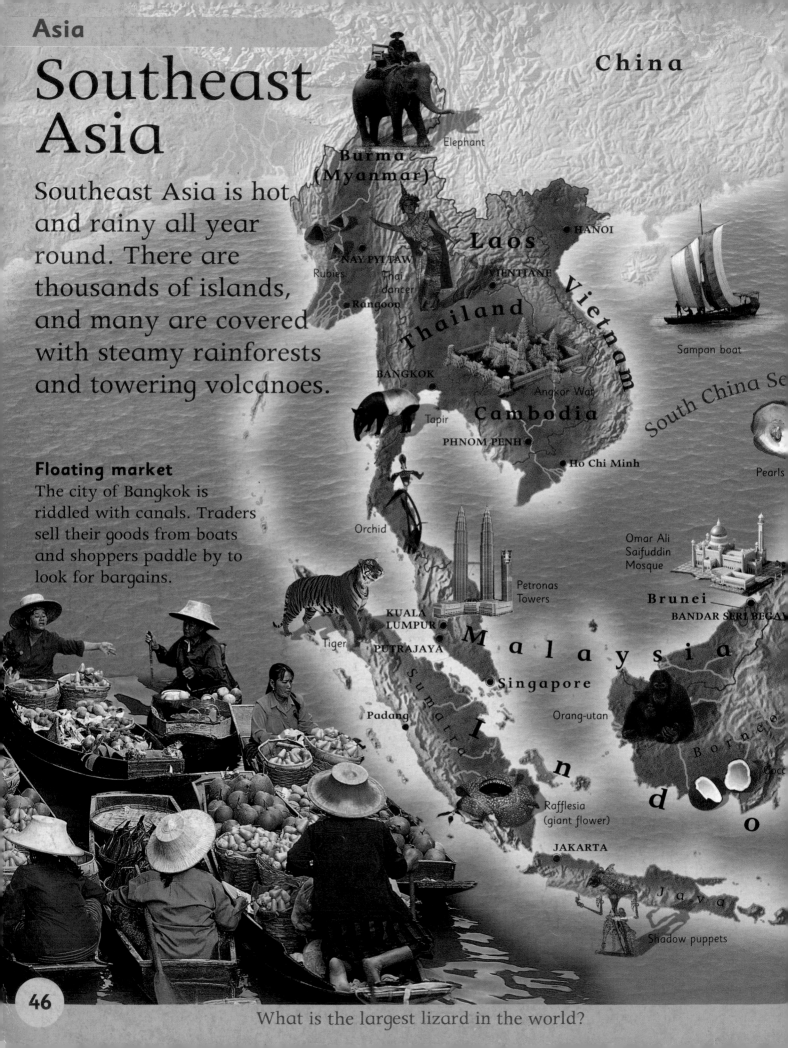

Southeast Asia

Southeast Asia is hot and rainy all year round. There are thousands of islands, and many are covered with steamy rainforests and towering volcanoes.

China

Elephant

Burma (Myanmar)

Rubies

NAY PYI TAW

Thai dancer

Rangoon

Thailand

HANOI

Laos

VIENTIANE

Vietnam

BANGKOK

Angkor Wat

Cambodia

Tapir

PHNOM PENH

Ho Chi Minh

Sampan boat

South China Sea

Pearls

Floating market

The city of Bangkok is riddled with canals. Traders sell their goods from boats and shoppers paddle by to look for bargains.

Orchid

Petronas Towers

KUALA LUMPUR

Tiger

PUTRAJAYA

M a l a y s i a

Omar Ali Saifuddin Mosque

Brunei

BANDAR SERI BEGAWAN

Sumatra

Singapore

Padang

Orang-utan

I n d o

Borneo

Rafflesia (giant flower)

JAKARTA

Java

Shadow puppets

46

Can you find...

A very rare kind of ape? **Orang-utans** live only in Borneo and Sumatra.

An animal with tusks that grow through its face? The **babirusa** is a kind of pig.

The world's largest flower? **Rafflesia** grows to nearly a metre (3 feet) wide.

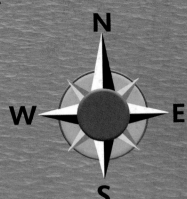

MANILA

Planting rice

Vinta boats

Philippines

Cebu

Water buffalo

Davao

Pacific Ocean

Tuna

Celebes Sea

Babirusa

Celebes

Toraja house

Moluccas

Nutmeg

Ambon

New Guinea

Jayapura

Conch shell

Asmat warrior

Papua New Guinea

PORT MORESBY

Mangoes

Komodo dragon

DILI
East Timor

Rice paddies

The wet climate is ideal for growing rice. Farmers plant it in flooded fields called paddies, which are sometimes built like steps in the sides of hills.

The Komodo dragon. It can grow to 3 m (10 ft) long.

China and neighbours

Over 1 billion people live in China – that's one-fifth of the world's people. Next door, Mongolia has the fewest people for its size.

Terracotta Army

This army of statues in Xi'an was made more than 2,000 years ago to guard the tomb of Qin Shi Huang, China's first emperor. The statues were rediscovered in 1974.

Chinese opera

Chinese opera has lots of singing, acting, and acrobatics. Make-up is used to show the type of character being played.

Altay

Mongolian ger (house)

Yining

Urumqi

Bact came

Turpan   Ham

Kashi

Ibex

▲ K2 8,611 m (28,250 ft)

Yak

Tibet

Potala Palace

Bhairabnath Temple

Himalayas

Lha

KATHMANDU
Mount Everest 8,850 m
(29,035 ft)   THIN

Nepal   Bhutan

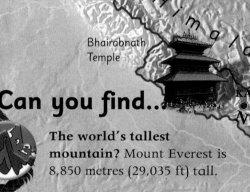

Can you find...

The world's tallest mountain? Mount Everest is 8,850 metres (29,035 ft) tall.

The world's most crowded place? Hong Kong has 6,000 people per square kilometre (16,500 per square mile).

China's hottest place? Turpan has recorded temperatures of up to 47°C (117°F).

What is the world's second tallest mountain?

Russian Federation

Mongolia

● ULAN BATOR

Dinosaur fossils

Gobi Desert

Snow sculptures at the
Harbin Ice Festival

● Harbin

● Jilin

● Shenyang

North Korea

● PYONGYANG

● SEOUL

Temple of Heaven

● Dalian

● BEIJING

South Korea

Seoul Olympic
Stadium

● Qingdao

Korea Strait

China

Great Wall of China

● Lanzhou

Tibetan monk

● Xi'an

Yellow River

Tea plantation

East China Sea

● Shanghai

● Hanzhou

Wuhan ●

River Yangtze

Junk (fishing boat)

Chengdu ●

China porcelain

● Changsha

Silk moth

Fuzhou ●

● Taipei

Taiwan

Hong Kong business district
and Exhibition Centre

Red panda

Electronic
goods

Kunming ●

Giant panda

● Hong Kong

● Nanning

Hainan

South China Sea

Japan

Japan is made up of four large islands and several thousand small ones. Most of the country is mountainous. The biggest cities are near the coast, where the land is flat.

Kurile Islands
(Russian Federation)

Steller's
sea eagle

Japanese
crane

Hokkaido

Pollock

Sapporo

Snow monkey

Aomori

Ou Mountains

Sushi

Cups for
rice wine

Honshu

Sea of Japan
(East Sea)

Snow and ice festival

An ice festival takes place every February in the town of Sapporo. People carve towers of ice into temples, sculptures, or replicas of famous buildings.

How many people live in Tokyo?

Robot dog

Toys and gadgets
Japan makes lots of electronic goods, such as computer games, televisions, and robot pets.

Kabuki theatre

Ogasawara Islands

Volcano Islands

Izu Islands

Pacific Ocean

Nagoya Castle

Pearl in shell

Mt Fuji 3776 m (12,389 ft)

Nagano

Kyoto

Osaka

Bullet train

Geishas

Honshu

Shinto shrine

Oki Islands

Chugoku

Hiroshima

Shikoku

Matsuyama castle

Sumo wrestlers

Bonsai tree

Iki

Fukuoka

Kyushu

Nagasaki

Octopus

East China Sea

Ryukyu Islands

Tokyo skyline
The capital city Tokyo is crowded and lively. Its skyscrapers are designed to sway slightly, which protects them from falling during earthquakes.

Sakishima Islands
These small tropical islands lie far to the south of the rest of Japan.

Ishigaki

Iriomote

Yonaguni

Okinawa

Australia

Australia is the world's smallest continent, but it is a huge country. Most Australians live on the coast, far from the vast, dusty deserts that make up the outback.

Poisonous animals

More poisonous animals live in Australia than in any other country.

The male **platypus** has a poisonous spur on each of its back ankles.

A **box jellyfish's** sting causes terrible pain that lasts for weeks and can kill.

Taipans are the world's deadliest snakes. A bite can kill in 30 minutes.

Sea snake venom can kill a child, but bites from these shy snakes are rare.

Cone shells are sea snails with deadly stings. The venom causes suffocation.

Funnel-web spiders have poisonous fangs. One bite can be fatal.

The tiny **blue-ringed octopus** can paralyse and kill a person with its bite.

Darwin

Saltwater crocodile

Boomerang

Broome

Dingo

Tanami Desert

Northern Territory

Port Hedland

Great Sandy Desert

Emu

Iron ore

Road train

Camel

Musgrav

Western Australia

Great Victoria Desert

South Australi

Kalgoorlie

Geraldton

Perth skyline

Perth
Fremantle

Kangaroo

Great Australian Bigh

Esperance

Great white shark

Albany

N
W   E
S

What is a coral reef made from?

Coral reef

The Great Barrier Reef stretches for 2,000 km (1,200 miles) along Queensland's coast. Many brightly coloured fish live on the reef.

Gulf of Carpentaria

Aboriginal paintings

Cape York Peninsula

Cairns

Great Barrier Reef

ennant Creek

The Devils Marbles

Mount Isa

Cattle farms

Townsville

Mackay

Rainbow lorikeet

Flying doctor

Queensland

Rockhampton

Alice Springs

impson Desert

Uluru (Ayers Rock)

Sheep stations

Koala

anges

Lake Eyre

Banana plantations

Pineapple farms

Brisbane

Opals

Coober Pedy

Broken Hill

Funnel-web spider

Sydney Opera House

Port Augusta

Whyalla

New South Wales

Sydney

Wollongong

Kookaburra

Adelaide

Wagga Wagga

Port Lincoln

Murray River

CANBERRA

Kangaroo Island

Victoria

Australian Capital Territory

Mount Gambier

Melbourne

Tram

Bass Strait

Tasmanian devil

Tasmania

Hobart

Sailing

53

New Zealand and the Pacific

Hundreds of islands are scattered across the Pacific Ocean. Two of the biggest form the mountainous country of New Zealand.

Extreme sports

New Zealand is the world capital for extreme sports. Bungee jumping, sky diving and white-water rafting are all popular.

Maori war dance

Most people in New Zealand are European, but about one in ten are Maoris – New Zealand's native people. On special occasions, Maoris paint their faces and perform a war dance called a haka.

Moving house

Earthquakes are common in New Zealand, so people live in wooden houses for safety. When people move home, they can carry their house away on a lorry.

Sheep shear

Kiwi

South Island

Aoraki (Mt. Cook) ▲
3,744 m (12,283 ft)

Christchurch

Takahe

Southern Alps

N e w

Rugby

Queenstown

Dunedin

Bungee jumping

Royal albatross

Sheep

Oysters

What's unusual about New Zealand's kiwi birds?

Red snapper

N **W** **E** **S**

Auckland

Pohuto geyser

Maori carving

Kiwi fruit

North Island

Parliament buildings
(Wellington)

WELLINGTON

Cook Strait

Sperm whale

Pacific
Ocean

Zealand

Coconut palms
Forests of coconut palms
grow along the beaches
of the Pacific islands.
Islanders climb these tall
trees to gather the coconuts.

Pacific islands
About 5 million people live
among the tropical islands
of the central Pacific.

Northern Mariana
Islands (USA)

Guam (USA)

Marshall
Islands

Palau

Micronesia

Papua New
Guinea

Nauru

Kiribati

Solomon
Islands

Tuvalu

Tokelau (NZ)

Wallis &
Futuna
(France)

Samoa

American
Samoa
(USA)

Cook Islands
(NZ)

Vanuatu

Tonga

Niue
(NZ)

Pacific
islanders fish from
small wooden
canoes.

New
Caledonia
(France)

Fiji

French
Polynesia
(France)

55

They can't fly.

Antarctica

The world's coldest continent is Antarctica, which is covered in ice. In winter it doubles in size as the sea freezes around it.

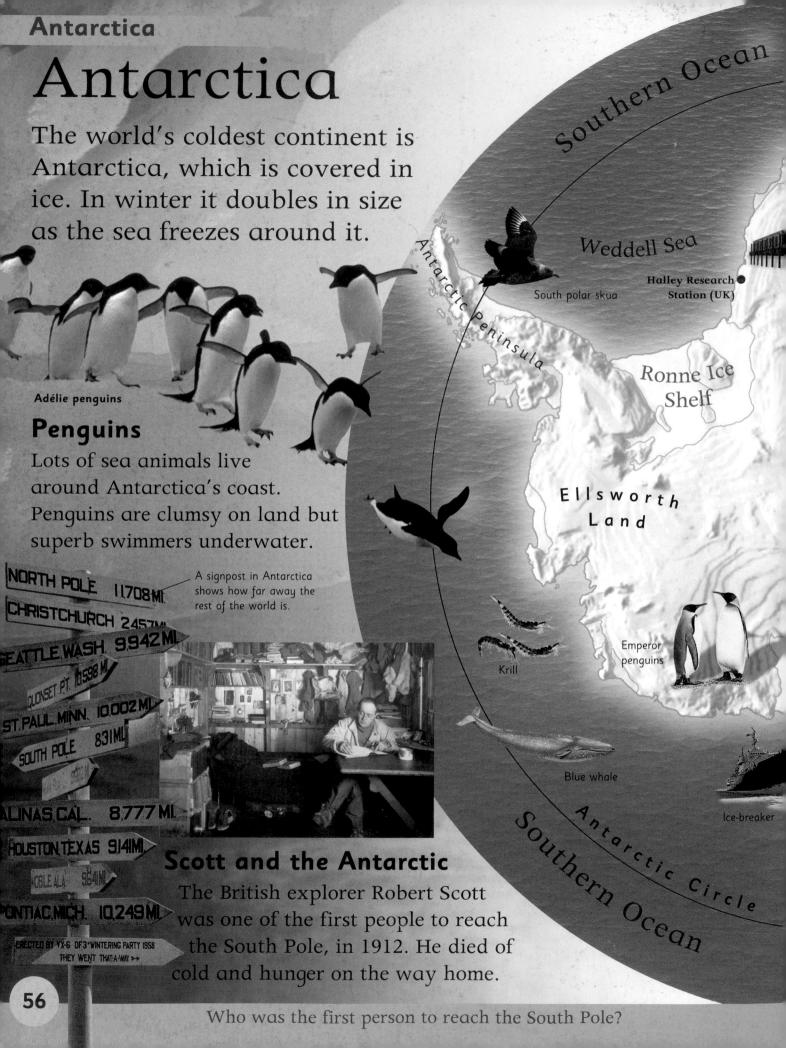

Adélie penguins

Penguins

Lots of sea animals live around Antarctica's coast. Penguins are clumsy on land but superb swimmers underwater.

A signpost in Antarctica shows how far away the rest of the world is.

NORTH POLE 11,708 MI.
CHRISTCHURCH 2457 MI.
SEATTLE,WASH. 9,942 MI.
QUONSET PT. 10,598 MI.
ST. PAUL, MINN. 10,002 MI.
SOUTH POLE 831 MI.
SALINAS, CAL. 8,777 MI.
HOUSTON, TEXAS 9,141 MI.
MOBILE, ALA. 9,641 MI.
PONTIAC, MICH. 10,249 MI.
ERECTED BY VX-6 OF 3 WINTERING PARTY 1958
THEY WENT THAT-A-WAY ➤➤

Scott and the Antarctic

The British explorer Robert Scott was one of the first people to reach the South Pole, in 1912. He died of cold and hunger on the way home.

Southern Ocean

Antarctic Peninsula

Weddell Sea

South polar skua

Halley Research Station (UK)

Ronne Ice Shelf

Ellsworth Land

Krill

Emperor penguins

Blue whale

Antarctic Circle

Southern Ocean

Ice-breaker

56

Who was the first person to reach the South Pole?

Right whale

Southern Ocean

Antarctic science

The only people who live in Antarctica are scientists. Some use huge balloons to study the climate on Antarctica.

Weather balloon.

Dronning Maud Land

Molodezhnaya Station (Russian Federation)

Adélie penguins

Survey plane

Antarctica

Princess Elizabeth Land

Amundsen-Scott Station (USA), South Pole

● SOUTH POLE

Snow mobile

Elephant seal

Vostok Station (Russian Federation)

Transantarctic Mountains

Life in the freezer

Antarctica is so cold that it freezes your breath into icicles around your mouth. People have to cover up in lots of very warm clothes.

Casey Station (Australia)

Ross Ice Shelf

● McMurdo Station (USA)

Ross Sea

Sno-cat

Icicles from breath.

Dumont d'Urville Station (France)

Snow petrel

Killer whale

Flags of the world

NORTH AND SOUTH AMERICA

Canada | United States of America | Mexico | Guatemala | Belize | Honduras | El Salvador | Nicaragua

St Kitts and Nevis | Dominica | St Lucia | St Vincent and The Grenadines | Barbados | Grenada | Trinidad and Tobago | Venezuela

AFRICA

Argentina | Paraguay | Uruguay | Morocco | Algeria | Tunisia | Libya | Egypt

Guinea-Bissau | Guinea | Sierra Leone | Liberia | Ivory Coast | Burkina | Ghana | Togo

Sao Tome and Principe | Gabon | Congo | Democratic Republic of Congo | Uganda | Rwanda | Burundi | Kenya

EUROPE

Swaziland | South Africa | Lesotho | Madagascar | Comoros | Cape Verde | Iceland | Norway

France | Monaco | Germany | Austria | Switzerland | Liechtenstein | Spain | Andorra | Portugal

Ukraine | Moldova | Poland | Czech Republic | Slovakia | Hungary | Slovenia | Croatia

RUSSIA AND CENTRAL ASIA

Cyprus | Russian Federation | Georgia | Azerbaijan | Armenia | Kazakhstan | Uzbekistan | Turkmenistan

Iraq | Kuwait | Saudi Arabia | Bahrain | Qatar | United Arab Emirates | Oman | Yemen

Vietnam | Cambodia | Philippines | Malaysia | Singapore | Brunei | Indonesia | East Timor

AUSTRALIA AND THE PACIFIC

Maldives | Mauritius | Seychelles | Australia | New Zealand | Palau | Micronesia | Marshall Islands

Which is the only country that doesn't have a rectangular flag?

There are 195 countries in the world. Each has its own flag.

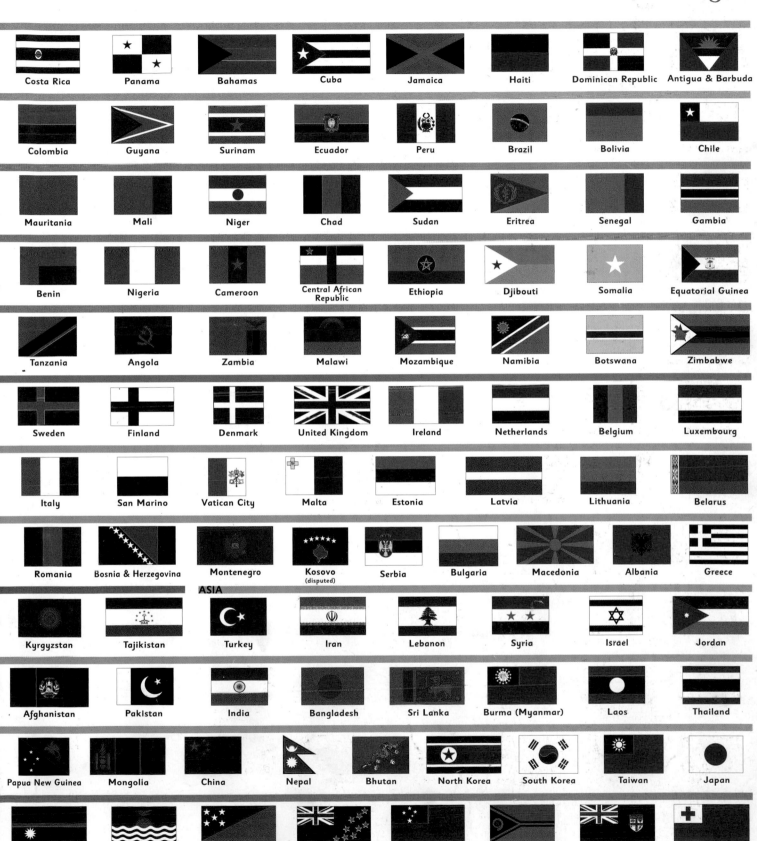

Costa Rica | Panama | Bahamas | Cuba | Jamaica | Haiti | Dominican Republic | Antigua & Barbuda

Colombia | Guyana | Surinam | Ecuador | Peru | Brazil | Bolivia | Chile

Mauritania | Mali | Niger | Chad | Sudan | Eritrea | Senegal | Gambia

Benin | Nigeria | Cameroon | Central African Republic | Ethiopia | Djibouti | Somalia | Equatorial Guinea

Tanzania | Angola | Zambia | Malawi | Mozambique | Namibia | Botswana | Zimbabwe

Sweden | Finland | Denmark | United Kingdom | Ireland | Netherlands | Belgium | Luxembourg

Italy | San Marino | Vatican City | Malta | Estonia | Latvia | Lithuania | Belarus

Romania | Bosnia & Herzegovina | Montenegro | Kosovo (disputed) | Serbia | Bulgaria | Macedonia | Albania | Greece

ASIA

Kyrgyzstan | Tajikistan | Turkey | Iran | Lebanon | Syria | Israel | Jordan

Afghanistan | Pakistan | India | Bangladesh | Sri Lanka | Burma (Myanmar) | Laos | Thailand

Papua New Guinea | Mongolia | China | Nepal | Bhutan | North Korea | South Korea | Taiwan | Japan

Nauru | Kiribati | Solomon Islands | Tuvalu | Samoa | Vanuatu | Fiji | Tonga

World of people

More than six billion people live in the world. These people have different customs, languages, beliefs, and lifestyles.

Language and people

One in every five people in the world lives in China. The most widely spoken language is Mandarin Chinese, which has almost one billion speakers.

This girl is dressed up for May Day – a festival that is celebrated in some parts of Europe.

Culture

People enjoy many different kinds of art and culture.

Writing is used to record information, news, views, stories, and history.

Theatre entertains audiences with acting, dance, and costume.

Painting is a way of expressing feelings and ideas through pictures.

Fashion is different all over the world, and is changing all the time.

Music styles can be classical or popular, traditional or modern.

May Day marks the first day of spring, after the long, cold months of winter.

Which is the second most spoken language in the world?

At work

All over the world, people work to earn a living. What job would you like to do? You could be an astronaut or a teacher, a farmer or a computer programmer.

At play

Having time for leisure and play is very important. Some people like watching or playing sport. Like these children, you might enjoy playing games with friends.

Celebrations

Important times in people's lives are celebrated with special feasts and festivals. These are times for people to enjoy themselves and to share their religious beliefs.

At some festivals in India, people exchange gifts of sweets, like these.

Curiosity quiz

Look through the People and Society pages and see if you can identify the picture clues below.

Become an expert

6-7 Our world
80-81 World of history

Spanish.

Religious lands

Many people follow a religion. A religion is a set of beliefs and a way of worship. The main religions today are Hinduism, Judaism, Buddhism, Christianity, Islam, and Sikhism.

Hinduism

Hinduism began in India about 4,000 years ago. Hindus believe in a spirit called Brahman (God). They also worship many gods and goddesses, who represent different parts of Brahman.

Hindus bathing in the holy River Ganges, in India

The Church of the Holy Sepulchre, in Jerusalem

Rosary

Sacred symbols

Each of these symbols has a special meaning.

Hinduism: the "Aum" symbol represents the first sound of creation.

Judaism: the Star of David reminds Jews of a great Jewish king.

Buddhism: the wheel represents eight points of the Buddha's teaching.

Christianity: the cross reminds Christians of Jesus' death on a cross.

Islam: the star and crescent moon appear on many Islamic flags.

Sikhism: the khanda symbol reminds Sikhs of God and of God's power.

Christianity

Christians follow the teachings of a man called Jesus Christ who lived about 2,000 years ago. They believe that Jesus was the son of God, who died to save them from sin.

What is the Christian holy book called?

This building is a Buddhist monastery in Thailand.

Islam

People who follow Islam are called Muslims. They believe in Allah (God), who guides them through their lives. The holy book of Islam is called the Qur'an (Koran). It contains the teachings of a prophet called Mohammed.

Mecca (Makkah) is a holy city for Muslims.

Western Wall

The Western Wall (Wailing Wall), in Jerusalem, is a holy place for Jews.

Buddhism

Buddhists follow the teachings of the Buddha. He was an Indian prince who lived about 2,500 years ago. He showed people how to live good, happy lives, full of peace.

Statues of the Buddha often show him meditating (thinking deeply).

Judaism

Judaism is the religion of the Jews. Their holy book is called the Torah. It tells the story of the Jewish people and their special relationship with God.

Menorah (Jewish candlestick)

Become an expert

The Golden Temple in Amritsar, India, is the holiest of all Sikh shrines.

Sikhism

The Sikh religion was started by a teacher called Guru Nanak. Sikhs worship in a building called a gurdwara. Their holy book is the Guru Granth Sahib.

Religious life

People honour their God or gods by following their teaching. They may come together for worship and celebrate special events with feasts and festivals.

Statue of
the Buddha

Islam
Muslims (followers of Islam) must pray five times a day: at dawn, midday, mid-afternoon, sunset, and night-time. Muslims follow a set of special prayer positions.

Buddhism
Buddhists do not worship a god, but honour the life and teachings of the Buddha. In the temple, they offer flowers, candles, and incense to the Buddha, to show their respect.

In some Buddhist countries, boys spend time as monks.

What is a mosque?

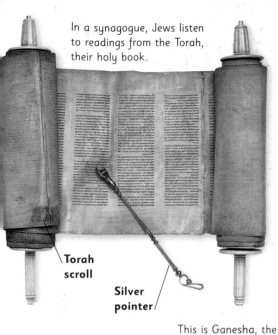

In a synagogue, Jews listen to readings from the Torah, their holy book.

Torah scroll

Silver pointer

Judaism

Jewish people meet to worship and pray in a special building called a synagogue. A man or woman called a rabbi leads the worship.

Turban

Small sword

Steel bangle

Sikhism

Many Sikh men wear five things to show their faith. These are uncut hair (often kept tidy in a turban), a wooden comb, a small sword, a steel bangle, and white undershorts.

This is Ganesha, the elephant-headed god.

Hinduism

Hindus worship the gods and goddesses in their homes and in mandirs (temples). The god Ganesha is said to bring good luck and success.

Christianity

Christmas is a joyful festival when Christians remember how Jesus was born. There are services in church, and people celebrate by exchanging cards and gifts.

Jesus was born in a stable in Bethlehem. Three kings brought presents for him.

These children are acting out the story of the first Christmas.

Joseph

Three kings

Jesus

Mary

A building where Muslims worship Allah (God).

Writing and printing

People began to write things down about 5,500 years ago. Before this, they told stories and passed news on by word of mouth. Today, writing is all around you.

The alphabet

— Fountain pens are filled with ink.

Quill pens in a pot of ink with a scroll made from papyrus reeds

Paper and pens

The paper you use today comes from trees. Long ago, people made paper from reeds or animal skins. The first pens were pieces of reeds, dipped in soot or ink.

Signs and symbols

Sometimes, signs and symbols are used to write letters and words, or even secret codes.

Pictograms are pictures used for writing. This old Chinese word means "to sell".

Hieroglyphs were used by the ancient Egyptians. This one stands for "chick".

Runes were Viking symbols that were carved on stone or wood. This is the "M" sound.

Music symbols like these are used to write down musical sounds (notes).

Morse code changes the alphabet into dot and dash signals for sending messages.

Writing machines

The first typewriters were invented about 200 years ago. They made writing much quicker. Today, word processors, like this laptop computer, are used instead.

Early typewriter   **Laptop computer**

What is a typeface?

Printing books

At first, books were written out by hand. This took a long time and was very costly. Printing presses, like the one shown here, were first used about 600 years ago. Printing books by machine was much quicker and cheaper.

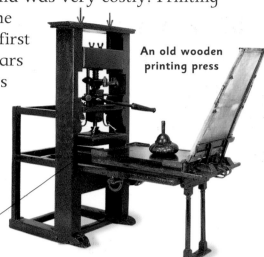

An old wooden printing press

The different parts of the machine were worked by hand.

Become an expert

84-85 Ancient Egypt

90-91 The Vikings

This machine sorts printed sheets into newspapers.

Printing the news

The first, hand-written newspapers date from Roman times. They told people about battles and gladiator contests. Today, giant rotary presses are used to print millions of books, newspapers, and magazines every day.

Every day, newspapers tell us what is happening in the world.

One rotary press can print more than 75,000 newspapers in one hour.

Herald INTERNATIONAL Tribune

LE FIG-ECO
premier quotidien économique français

EL PAIS

Art and architecture

Since ancient times, artists have painted pictures and used stone and wood to make sculptures. Architects plan the world's buildings.

Cave painting
Prehistoric artists painted pictures of figures and animals on cave walls. This cave art is from the USA.

Church art
The Italian artist Michelangelo painted scenes from the Bible on the ceiling and walls of the Sistine Chapel in Rome, Italy.

Modern sculpture
Modern British artist Henry Moore used bold shapes to create this interesting – and "touchable" – giant stone sculpture.

Architecture can change the way a whole city looks.

Singapore skyline

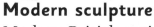

Skyscraper

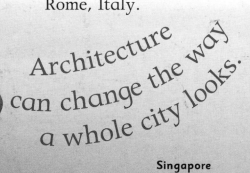

When was the Sydney Opera House opened?

Architecture

Every building you see has been planned by an architect. Styles of architecture have changed over thousands of years. Buildings are designed for living, working, worship, or simply for fun.

Castles were built to defend people from attack. This castle is in Spain.

The Taj Mahal

The beautiful Taj Mahal in India was built as a tomb for the emperor's wife. It is made from white marble set with coloured stones.

Modern skyscrapers make up the Singapore skyline.

Making art

People use different types of art to capture a scene or express their ideas. Here are a few of them.

Drawing a quick "sketch" in pencil is a way for artists to plan a colour painting.

Painting in colour is often done on a canvas using watercolour or oil paints.

Sculpture is the skill of making artistic shapes out of stone, wood, or metal.

Photography is a very accurate way of showing how people and places look.

Graphic design is a way of combining pictures and words in imaginative ways.

An opera house

The Opera House in Sydney, Australia, is a modern building. Its wing-like roof makes it easy to identify. It was designed to look like the sails of boats in the nearby harbour.

Become an expert

In 1973.

Music

What is your favourite song or tune? Do you like classical, jazz, folk, rock, or pop music? If you play a musical instrument, you can make music of your own.

Conductor

An orchestra

Some musicians perform together in a group called an orchestra. There are about 90 musicians in a symphony orchestra. The conductor keeps them in time. Orchestras usually play classical music.

Drums and cymbals are percussion instruments.

Cymbal

Drum

Musical instruments

In an orchestra, there are four kinds of instruments — brass, woodwind, percussion, and strings. Each instrument makes its own individual sound. The different sounds blend together.

Flute

What sort of instrument is a xylophone?

Recording music

In a recording studio, each voice or instrument can be recorded on its own. These are called tracks. Engineers mix the tracks together.

Mixing desk

The knobs on the mixing desk control the volume and tone of each track.

Types of music

Many different kinds of music are played all over the world.

Early music was probably played on instruments made from animal bones.

Opera is a play set to music in which the performers sing their lines.

Jazz musicians make up some or all of the music as they play it.

Rock music, or rock and roll, has punchy lyrics (words) and a strong beat.

Pop is short for popular music. It has catchy tunes and is good for dancing to.

Madonna is one of the most successful pop singers of all time.

Madonna

Vinyl record

CDs

Tape

Music can be recorded in many ways: on computers, MP3 players, CDs, vinyl records, and tapes.

Many rock and pop musicians play music on electric guitars.

Pop concerts

Watching your favourite pop star perform live on stage can be thrilling. Many people work behind the scenes to make the show run smoothly.

Cello

French horn

Piano keyboard

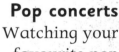
Hands on

Would you like to be a pop star? Try writing your own pop song. Start by writing a poem, then make up a tune to go with it.

A percussion instrument.

Theatre and dance

Theatre began thousands of years ago in ancient Greece. Actors and dancers put on shows to entertain and inform people.

Actors and acting

Putting on a play is a long task. First, the playwright writes the play. Then actors bring the story and the characters in the play to life. They also have to remember their words!

Actors use their body, as well as the words, to create a character and perform the scenes.

These actors are playing two characters called Romeo and Juliet.

Costumes help to show when and where the play's action is happening.

Musical theatre

Going to the theatre to see a musical is a special treat. Musicals are an exciting mixture of acting, dancing, and song. This is a scene from the musical "Oliver!".

Who wrote the play "Romeo and Juliet"?

Japanese theatre

These actors are performing an ancient type of Japanese play, called Kabuki. They wear beautiful costumes and mix acting, singing, dancing, and music to put on a dazzling show.

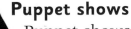

Indian dance

Dancing is a way of telling a story or showing a feeling using movement and music. This type of dancing, from India, is made up of special movements and expressions.

Forms of dance

There are many different types and styles of dance from all over the world.

Tap dancers wear metal-capped shoes to make "tap" sounds.

Ballet is a graceful type of dance, set to music, that tells a tale.

Country and **folk** dances from around the world are lively and fun.

Flamenco is a dramatic Spanish dance set to the sound of clicking castanets.

Jazz dance uses the rhythm and beat of jazz music to create an exciting dance.

Puppet shows

Puppet shows are a very old type of theatre. These glove puppets are simple to work. A hand inside makes the puppet move. One finger works the puppet's head, while two other fingers work the arms.

Punch

Judy

Become an expert

70-71 Music

86-87 Ancient Greece

Punch and Judy are famous puppets from Britain.

William Shakespeare.

Clothes and fashion

What are you wearing today? A T-shirt? Trousers? Trainers? Clothes can make you look good. They may also have a special job to do.

Types of fabric

Cotton is made of fibres from the cotton plant. The fabric is usually woven.

Silk is a thin, soft fabric made from threads spun by silkworms.

Leather is made from the skins of animals such as cows.

Wool is made from the hair of sheep. It is often knitted to make clothes.

Nylon and other artificial fabrics are made from chemicals.

This Vietnamese boy is wearing casual clothes.

This Indian girl is wearing a sari.

A raincoat, Wellington boots, and umbrella are useful when it rains.

This French girl wears a top and skirt for school.

What do you wear?

What you wear depends on where you live and what you are doing. People wear different clothes for keeping warm, staying cool, for playing sport, and for going to school.

What is a beret ("ber-reh")?

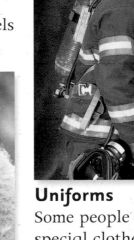

Fashion shows
Some people design clothes to look stylish or unusual. They are called fashion designers. They put on fashion shows where models show off their clothes.

Clothes for the cold
In cold climates, clothes were traditionally made from animal fur and skins. Today, synthetic (artificial) fabrics are often used instead.

Uniforms
Some people have to wear special clothes for work. These are called uniforms. This fire-fighter's uniform protects against heat and flames. Do you wear a uniform at school?

This beautiful outfit is the national dress of a hill tribe from Vietnam.

This girl is wearing a kimono, the national dress of Japan.

This Masai girl from Tanzania is wearing her colourful national dress.

Children from the Arctic need thick, fur-lined clothes for warmth.

National dress
A country's traditional clothes are called its national dress. In many countries, people only wear their national dress for festivals or other special occasions.

A round, flat type of hat.

Working people

What do you want to be when you grow up? All over the world, people do different kinds of work to earn the money to buy their food, clothes, and homes.

Astronauts

Astronauts are people who work in space. Some fly spacecraft. Others do science experiments in space. The astronauts in this picture are working inside a Space Shuttle.

Market sellers

There are markets selling food and other goods in almost every town and city. This man is selling fruit and vegetables from his market stall in Cairo, Egypt.

What do you call someone who writes books to earn a living?

This vet is giving a cat a health check.

The farmer's plough is being pulled by an ox.

Vets

If your pet is ill, you take it to the vet. Vets look after sick and injured animals. Some vets treat small animals, such as cats and dogs. Others work with farm or zoo animals.

Farmers

All over the world, farmers grow crops and raise animals. They grow food for themselves and to sell at market. This farmer is ploughing his rice field in Thailand.

Teachers

This teacher is helping some children to learn to read.

Who is your favourite teacher? At school, teachers help you to learn science, languages, and other subjects. Teachers have to go to college to learn how to teach you!

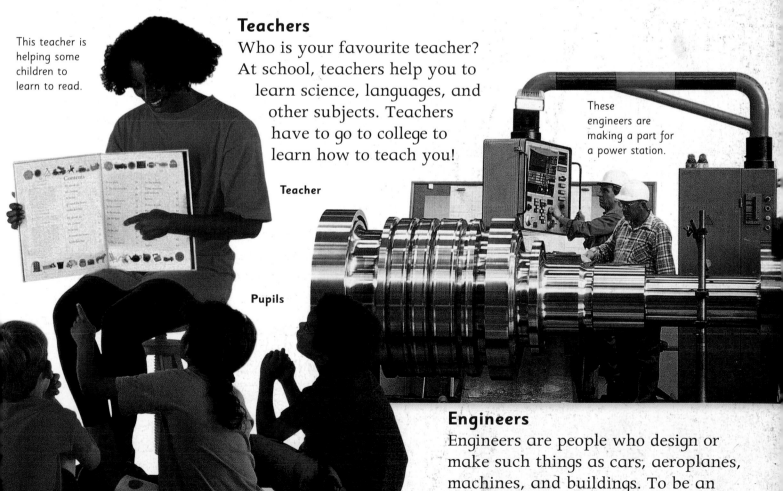

Teacher

Pupils

These engineers are making a part for a power station.

Engineers

Engineers are people who design or make such things as cars, aeroplanes, machines, and buildings. To be an engineer, you need to be good at science and mathematics.

An author.

79

World of history

History tells us the story of how people lived in the past. From the things they left behind, we can find out about their homes, food, clothes, work, and beliefs.

The mummy mask of the Egyptian king, Tutankhamun

Decorative blue stones called lapis lazuli

Solid gold

Early people

About 10,000 years ago, groups of people began to settle down in certain places. They started to farm the land and to raise animals for food.

Early farmers cut down the ripe wheat stalks with a sickle made from a sharp flint stone set in a wooden handle.

People learnt how to grow crops for food.

Powerful kings

Many great civilizations were ruled by powerful kings. In ancient Egypt, the kings were called pharaohs. They were so important that people worshipped them as gods.

Spanish galleon

80

Where did the Aztecs and Incas live?

Greeks and Romans

About 2,500 years ago, ancient Greek culture flourished. Then the Romans grew in strength and ruled over a great empire from Rome in present-day Italy.

The ancient Acropolis in Athens, Greece

Explorers

For centuries, people have travelled far and wide across the world. They went in search of new lands, goods to trade, and adventures.

These coins were made by European explorers using the gold they discovered on their travels.

Now people are exploring space.

The first Space Shuttle flight was made in 1981 with a Shuttle called Columbia.

20th century

The 20th century saw many new inventions and discoveries being made. People flew in space for the first time, and even walked on the Moon.

Curiosity quiz

Look through the History of People pages and see if you can identify the picture clues below.

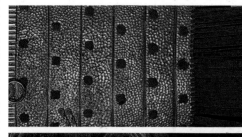

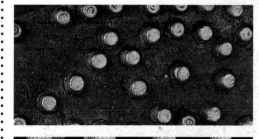

Become an expert

66-67 Writing and printing
280-281 Men on the moon

In Central and South America.

From apes to human beings

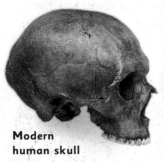

Homo habilis skull

Neanderthal skull

Modern human skull

Our oldest ancestors looked like apes. Slowly, they became more human-like and began to walk upright on two legs.

Early people

The first human beings lived about two million years ago. We do not know exactly what they looked like, but we do know how they lived.

Cave shelters

Early people used caves like these as shelters. Inside, the caves were safe and warm. Sometimes, people painted the walls with pictures of the animals they hunted.

The first farmers

Until 10,000 years ago, people had to travel in search of food. Then they began to grow crops and keep animals for meat and milk. These people were the first farmers.

Fire

Flint blade

A flint hand axe from Egypt.

Tools and fire

We take fire and tools for granted, but early people had to learn how to make and use them. The first tools were stone hand axes, made about 600,000 years ago.

This woman is grinding grain between two stones to make flour for bread.

How did early people start fires?

The first cities
When people started growing their food, they were able to settle in one place. They began to build houses, villages, and cities. One of the first cities was Jericho in Jordan.

Hunters and gatherers
Early people hunted woolly mammoths, cave bears, reindeer, and other animals for food. They also collected fruit, nuts, and roots, and caught fish.

The meat from a mammoth was enough to feed a family for a whole year.

Mammoth hunting was dangerous work!

Early inventions
Here are some of the everyday things that early people used.

Dogs were first used for hunting about 10,000 years ago.

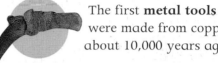

The first **metal tools** were made from copper about 10,000 years ago.

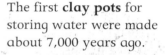

The first **clay pots** for storing water were made about 7,000 years ago.

Become an expert
92-93 Aztecs, Incas, and Mayas

Hunters killed the mammoth with wooden spears.

By rubbing two sticks or striking two stones together.

Ancient Egypt

The ancient Egyptians lived by the banks of the River Nile about 3,500 years ago. Their powerful rulers were called pharaohs.

Beautifully decorated mummy

The pyramids

The ancient Egyptians believed in life after death. The pharaohs built magnificent tombs for themselves, called pyramids.

Mummy of a cat

Building skills

Egyptian builders did not have modern tools and machines to help them. The workers carried huge stone blocks into place, or sent them on barges along the river.

These men are carrying stone blocks for building, as the ancient Egyptians did.

Mummification

When an important person died, the body was "mummified". Some of the inside parts were removed. Then the body was treated with chemicals and wrapped in bandages.

Hands on

Try writing out a message using only Egyptian hieroglyphics. You could also make up your own set of hieroglyphic symbols.

Why did the Egyptians mummify their dead?

The Nile floods

Each year, the River Nile flooded and spread rich, black soil on its banks. Farmers grew crops in the soil and used the river water to water their fields.

The River Nile in Egypt

A funeral barge

Nile barges were important for transport.

Hieroglyphics

The Egyptians used picture writing called hieroglyphics. Symbols, such as those below, stood for letters and sounds.

Hieroglyphic sound chart

ah	b	c, k	d
ee, y	f	g	h
kh	m	n	p
r	s	t	oo, u, w

The mysterious Sphinx still stares out across the desert.

The great Sphinx guards the pyramid of a pharaoh called Khafra.

The Sphinx

A huge stone statue, called the Sphinx, guards the pyramids at Giza. It has the body of a lion and a human head, which was modelled on the pharaoh's own features.

To keep the body whole for the next life.

Ancient Greece

About 2,500 years ago, Greece was made up of powerful "city-states", suc as Athens and Sparta, which fought wars against each other.

Greek buildings

The ancient Greeks built beautiful temples where they worshipped their gods. This temple in Athens was built to honour the goddess Athena.

Greek theatre

Going to the theatre was very popular in ancient Greece. The Greeks wrote many plays, including tragedies and comedies. People watched their favourite plays in large outdoor theatres, like the one above.

Where were the first Olympic Games held?

The Trojan War

During a long war with the city of Troy, the Greeks gave the Trojans a huge wooden horse as a gift. But the horse was full of soldiers, who attacked the Trojans as they slept.

These soldiers were called hoplites.

Helmet with nose protector

Strong, bronze metal armour protected the body.

Warriors

Each city had an army, and war was part of daily life. Soldiers had to buy their own weapons and armour, so they often came from rich families.

These leg guards are called greaves.

Greek mythology

The Greeks told many stories about their gods and goddesses.

 Zeus was king of the gods and chief of the 12 gods who lived on Mount Olympus.

 Athena was goddess of war, wisdom, and Athens. She helped heroes in battle.

 Poseidon was the brother of Zeus and Hades and god of the seas and earthquakes.

 Aphrodite was goddess of love and beauty. She loved Ares, the god of war.

Hades was god of the Underworld – the home of the dead in Greek legends.

Shield

Some shields were decorated with crests.

In Olympia, Greece.

The Romans

Ancient Rome began as a group of small villages along the River Tiber in Italy. It soon grew into a great and powerful city that ruled a mighty empire.

The Forum

The city of Rome

The city of Rome is still a busy place, just as it was in ancient times. If you visit Rome today, you can see the ruins of the Forum, the Colosseum, and many other splendid Roman buildings.

Gladiators

The Colosseum was a huge building in Rome where people went to watch wild beast shows and gladiator fights. Gladiators often fought to the death.

Gladiators were armed with nets and spears, or small shields and swords.

50,000 people could sit and watch the fights in the arena.

Lions and other wild animals were killed during the shows.

What was a Roman villa?

Latin language

The Romans spoke a language called Latin. Roman children learnt to write Latin by scratching out letters on wooden boards that were covered in wax.

This inscription is written in Latin.

The Roman Empire

The Romans conquered a vast empire. They built this wall between Scotland and England to protect the boundary of their empire.

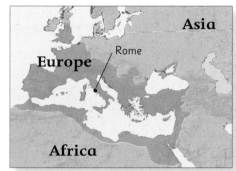

Asia

Rome

Europe

Africa

The purple area on this map shows the size of the Roman Empire in about 300 CE.

Hadrian's Wall

Famous Romans

Below, you can read about some of the most famous Romans of all.

Spartacus was a slave who led an army of slaves against the Romans.

Julius Caesar was a great general who ruled Rome. He was murdered.

Augustus was the first Roman emperor. After his death, he was made a god.

Ovid was a Roman poet. He wrote many poems about myths and legends.

Hadrian toured the empire and built walls and forts to guard it.

The Roman army

The Romans had the best army in the world. Their soldiers conquered many countries and guarded the empire. The soldiers often had to march long distances.

A soldier's sandals

A standard (army flag)

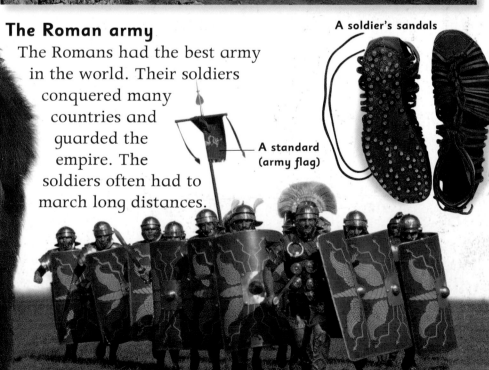

Roman roads

In peacetime, Roman soldiers were kept busy building roads. Roads were important for moving the army around the empire. Roman roads were usually very straight. Some are still used today.

A large house in the countryside.

The Vikings

The Vikings lived more than 1,000 years ago. Their home was in Scandinavia, in northern Europe, but they are famous for their long sea journeys to distant lands.

Mast

The sail was made from wool or linen.

Longships

Viking boats were called longships. They were built from wood, and were fast and strong enough to cover vast distances.

Ropes

Viking travellers

The Vikings were daring sailors and explorers. They made fierce raids on the countries of western Europe. They went in search of trade and new lands to live in – even as far away as North America.

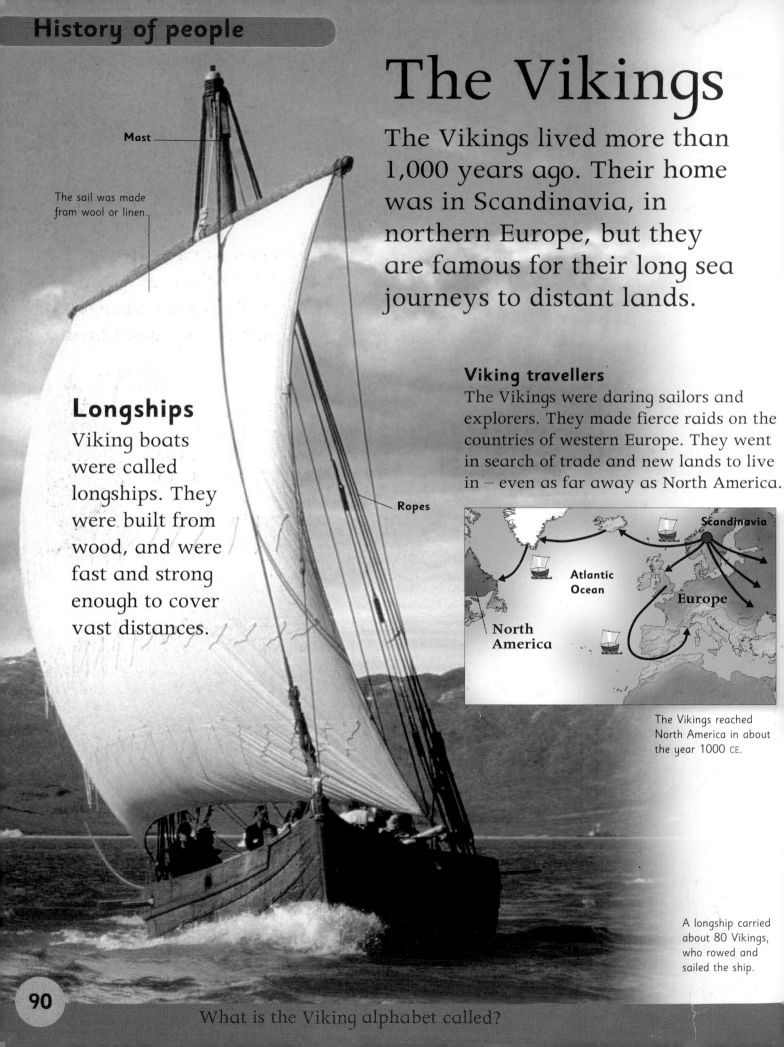

Scandinavia

Atlantic Ocean

Europe

North America

The Vikings reached North America in about the year 1000 CE.

A longship carried about 80 Vikings, who rowed and sailed the ship.

What is the Viking alphabet called?

Warrior duty

Being a brave warrior was very important to the Vikings. They could be called up to fight at any moment, so they always dressed ready for battle.

Iron and wood spear

Viking warriors carried wooden shields and wore armour made from leather or chain mail.

Helmet with noseguard

Chain-mail shirt

Viking homes

Viking families lived in houses made from wood, stone, or turf. A hole was left in the roof to let out smoke from the cooking fire. People sat on stools or benches around the fire and slept on raised beds.

A small statue of a Viking god called Frey

Story-telling

To entertain each other, the Vikings told long stories about their heroes, gods, and great warriors. The stories were called sagas.

Runes

The Vikings carved poems and inscriptions using symbols called runes. Each rune was made of straight lines, so it was easy to carve them on wood or stone.

Swords and spears were used for fighting.

Round wooden shield

Long woollen socks

Iron sword

Goat-skin shoes

It is called "Futhark" ("foo-thark").

Aztecs, Incas, and Mayas

Three great civilizations grew up in the ancient Americas. They were called the Aztecs, Mayas, and Incas. These people built great cities and temples to their gods.

Aztec warrior headdress

Where did they live?

The Aztecs and Mayas ruled large parts of Mexico and Central America. The Inca Empire stretched along the west coast of South America.

Aztecs
Mayas
Incas

Aztec temple

Aztec temples looked like pyramids, with steps leading to a shrine on top. Here, the Aztecs killed people and offered their hearts to the god of the Sun.

This is Chicomecoatl, the Aztec goddess of maize.

Gods and farming

The Aztecs prayed to the gods to make their crops grow. Most important was maize (corn). It was ground into flour for making flat breads called tortillas.

How were the Incas like the ancient Egyptians?

Spanish galleon

Spanish invasion

In the 16th century, Spanish explorers came to the Americas. Their arrival meant the end of the Aztec, Maya, and Inca empires. Many people were killed and their cities destroyed.

Inca gold

The Incas made objects from gold. The Spanish greed for gold led to the end of the Inca empire.

Llamas were important to the Incas. They were used for wool and for transport.

Gold armbands may have been worn by the bravest Inca warriors.

Statues of Inca gods were made from gold to show honour towards them.

Mayan cities

The Maya built great cities, filled with magnificent stone temples, palaces, and squares. This is the Temple of the Great Jaguar in the Mayan city of Tikal.

Tikal is in Guatemala, South America.

Hands on

Make an Aztec headdress. Cut a strip of card to go round your head and stick on card feathers. Paint it and tape the ends together.

Inca farmers

This is the Inca city of Machu Picchu, high in the Andes mountains in Peru. Farmers grew crops in level fields cut into the mountainside. Maize, legumes (beans), and squash were their main crops.

Ruins of Machu Picchu's buildings can still be seen in Peru today.

They made mummies.

Types of castle

The first castles were made from wood, but stone was stronger.

French chateaux were magnificent royal homes, with moats and towers.

Norman keeps were stone towers, surrounded by thick castle walls.

Japanese castles were built by warrior lords and had decorative roofs.

The **Red Fort** in India was a palace with stone walls 30 m (100 ft) tall.

Knights and castles

Even for brave knights in the middle ages, attacking a castle was dangerous. Thick walls kept them out, and the castle archers had their bows and arrows ready.

Castle design

Massive walls and towers made castles almost impossible for enemy soldiers to attack. Many castles were built on hills, so they were difficult to reach.

Hands on

Make a knight's shield from a big piece of coloured card. Decorate the shield with your own coat of arms, cut out of silver paper.

Battlements

Tower

Thick walls

Jousting

In peacetime, knights fought practice battles, called jousts, to train for war. They used poles (lances) to knock each other off their horses.

What was chain mail?

Helmet

Knights

Knights were soldiers who fought on horseback. They wore heavy armour made from iron and were armed with axes, swords, and spears.

A knight used his sword to stab between the gaps in an enemy's armour.

Leg guard (greave)

Spur

Samurai warriors

In Japan, knights were called samurai. They were warriors who fought for a powerful lord and followed a strict code of honour.

Buffalo horns

Samurai warriors wore armour made from coated wood or plates of metal laced together.

Leather leg protector

Samurai sword

Archers fired arrows through slits in the walls.

Lance

Each knight had his own pattern, called his coat of arms.

Shield

Portcullis

Moat

95

Armour made from small loops of metal.

20th century

The 20th century was the time from 1901 to 2000. In the 20th century there were many events, inventions, and discoveries that changed people's lives for ever.

British air force symbol

A British fighter aircraft from World War II

World wars

There were two terrible world wars during the 20th century. World War I lasted from 1914 to 1918. World War II lasted from 1939 to 1945. Millions of soldiers and civilians died in these wars.

Nuclear power

The first nuclear power station was opened in 1954. Today, there are about 400 of them in the world. These power stations make dangerous waste. Some people think they should be closed down.

Nearly three-quarters of France's electricity is made at nuclear power stations. This one is on the River Seine.

This is Sirius, a ship owned and used by the Greenpeace organization.

Thick armour protects the tank.

The tracks stop the heavy tank sinking into mud.

Tank

Who was the first person to go into space? And when?

Pop music

The Beatles were one of the most successful pop groups of all time. In the 1960s, millions of people bought their records. Performances on television also helped to boost their fame. The Beatles split up in 1970.

The Beatles playing live on television in New York, USA

Man on the Moon

In 1969, astronauts visited the Moon for the first time. People all around the world watched on television as the astronauts stepped onto the Moon's grey, dusty surface.

Buzz Aldrin

Buzz Aldrin was the second man on the Moon.

Space suit

Advances

Advances made in the 20th century have made many people's lives easier.

 Mobile telephones and the **Internet** make it easy to keep in touch.

 Medical advances help us to fight diseases and recover from injuries.

 Inventions such as the jet engine have made travel fast and cheap.

 Sport became extremely popular, and many sports people became very famous.

 Scientific discoveries, such as DNA, helped medicine and technology.

The environment

Some people began to worry about the damage that humans are doing to the environment. They formed organizations such as Greenpeace and Friends of the Earth.

Nelson Mandela

There were many important political changes during the 20th century. Nelson Mandela fought against an unfair political system in South Africa. He became president of South Africa in 1994.

Technology

Many new types of technology were developed in the 20th century. Microchips were invented in the 1950s. They are used in computers, televisions, stereos, and many other machines.

A Russian cosmonaut (astronaut) called Yuri Gagarin in 1961.

Your amazing body

The greatest machine you'll ever own is your body. It's more complicated than any computer, it lasts for a lifetime, and it's yours for free.

Become an expert.

106-107 Bones and muscles

116-117 Eating and digestion

Body parts

Your body is made up of hundreds of different parts. You probably know the names of the bits you can see, but there are many more hidden deep inside you.

Inside your body

Doctors can see inside your body with special cameras. X-ray cameras take pictures of hard body parts like bones. Other cameras, called scanners, can see soft body parts.

Hair

Forehead

Ears

Eyebrows

Cheeks

Nose

Eyes

Lips

Teeth

Hands

Wrists

Fingers

Two of everything

Body parts often come in pairs. You have two feet, two eyes, two ears, two lungs, and so on. This means you have a handy spare in case one of them gets damaged.

A chest X-ray shows the bones in your chest. The white shape in the middle is the heart.

What do we call the study of the human body?

Water, water

Your body is mostly water – it makes up about two-thirds of your weight.

Curiosity quiz

Take a look at the pages in this section and see if you can find these pictures.

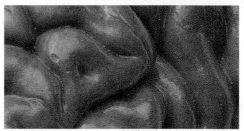

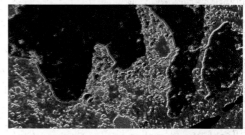

Robot

No substitute

The human body is too complicated for robots to copy. Robots can copy the way we walk, but they can't think or feel like we do.

The ingredients

Your body is made of just a few simple chemicals, plus water.

Carbon is what diamonds and coal are made of. A fifth of you is carbon.

Iron makes your blood red. You have enough to make one small iron nail.

Phosphorus is in the tips of matches, as well as your bones and teeth.

Sodium and **chlorine** make salt. Blood is one-third as salty as sea water.

Potassium is used in some types of soap. It's also in your body fluids.

Nitrogen is important in muscles. It's also the main ingredient in air.

Chimps have hands like ours.

Compared to chimps, our bodies look almost hairless.

Chimpanzee

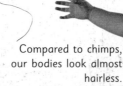

Being human

Although we look different from animals, our bodies are similar on the inside. Our closest animal relatives are chimpanzees.

What makes you you?

All human bodies work the same way, but everyone is different. Nobody looks, sounds, or thinks exactly like you. You're different because of the way your genes and experience shape you as you grow up.

Fair skin

Green eyes

Curly hair

Black hair

Unique
The shape of your face, the colour of your hair, and many other things make you unique – different from everyone else.

Freckles

How many genes are there in each cell in the human body?

In the genes

Genes are instructions that build your body and tell it how to work. Your genes control many of the things that make you unique, like the colour of your eyes or how tall you'll be.

This girl has a gene that allows her to roll up her tongue. The boy doesn't have the gene, so he can't do it.

There's enough DNA inside you to stretch to the Sun and back 400 times.

DNA

Your genes are stored in a chemical called DNA, which looks like a twisted ladder with four different types of rung. The rungs make up a four-letter alphabet that spells out your genes, like letters in a book.

DNA can split and copy itself.

Hands on

Look in a mirror and see if you can roll your tongue. Don't cheat by squeezing it with your lips. Test your family to see who has the gene.

Learning to ride a bike changes your brain and your body.

Changing body

Genes don't control everything – experience also shapes you. If you exercise a lot, for instance, your body gets stronger.

In the family

Your genes came from your parents. Half come from your mother and half come from your father. If you look like your parents, it's because you share the same genes.

About 30,000 specific genes.

Building blocks

Every part of your body is made of tiny building blocks called cells, which fit together like bricks in a wall. Cells are so small that hundreds could fit on the point of a pin.

The nucleus controls the rest of the cell.

DNA is stored in the cell nucleus.

DNA

The inside of a cell is packed with a kind of living jelly called cytoplasm.

The skin on your fingertips is made of lots of small ridges.

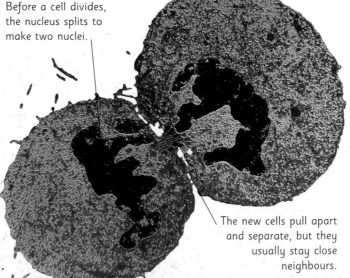

Inside a cell

In the middle of a cell is its control centre – the nucleus. The nucleus sends instructions to the rest of the cell, telling the cell what chemicals to make.

The outer skin, or membrane, stops things leaking out.

Tiny generators provide cells with power.

Before a cell divides, the nucleus splits to make two nuclei.

Making new cells

A cell makes new cells by dividing. The two new cells are half the size, but they soon grow back. Millions of your cells die every second, but millions of others divide to replace them.

The new cells pull apart and separate, but they usually stay close neighbours.

How many cells are there in the human body?

How big are cells?

Cells are too small to see with the naked eye, but scientists can photograph them through powerful microscopes. The cells on your skin are about a hundredth of a millimetre wide.

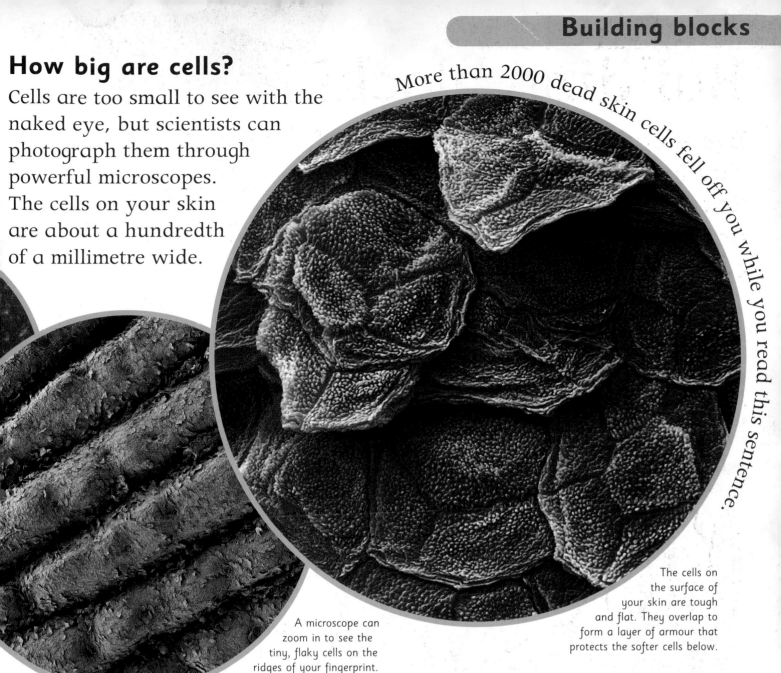

More than 2000 dead skin cells fell off you while you read this sentence.

A microscope can zoom in to see the tiny, flaky cells on the ridges of your fingerprint.

The cells on the surface of your skin are tough and flat. They overlap to form a layer of armour that protects the softer cells below.

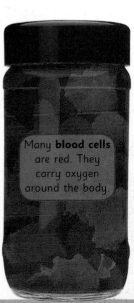

Fat cells are bubble shaped. They store fat under your skin.

Many **blood cells** are red. They carry oxygen around the body.

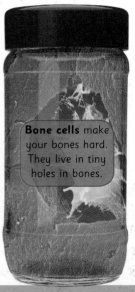

Nerve cells are thin and wiry. They carry electrical signals.

Bone cells make your bones hard. They live in tiny holes in bones.

Cells make tissue

Your body contains hundreds of different types of cells that do different jobs. Cells of the same type usually group together to form tissue. Fat, muscle, bone, and nerves are types of tissue. Blood is a liquid tissue.

About 100 trillion.

Organizing the body

Your cells and tissues are organized into larger body parts called organs. In turn, your organs work together to form body systems.

Systems

Organs and tissues work in teams to carry out major tasks, like transporting blood or processing food. These teams are called systems.

The heart is the largest organ in the blood system. It pumps blood around the body.

Heart

Kidney

Brain

Organs

An organ is a body part that does a specific job. Your heart's job, for instance is to pump blood. Kidneys clean blood.

The tubes that carry blood away from the heart are called arteries (shown in red).

The tubes that carry blood back to the heart are called veins (shown in blue).

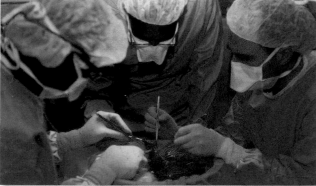

Organ transplant

If a vital organ stops working, doctors may replace it with an organ from another person. This is called a transplant.

Heart and blood

Your heart, blood, and blood vessels make up the blood system. It transports vital supplies around your body.

Which body system makes your stomach rumble?

Muscles

Your muscle system is made of tissues that move parts of your body by pulling on them or squeezing them. Your biggest muscles all pull on bones.

Muscles change the position of your skeleton by pulling different bones.

Your fingers are moved by muscles in your arm.

The most powerful muscles are in your legs.

Skeleton

Bones and joints make up the skeletal system, an inner frame that supports the body.

A quarter of your bones are in your feet.

Nerves

Your nervous system carries electrical signals around your body. You need this system to see, hear, think, and react.

Signals shoot along nerves to muscles, telling them when to pull.

Senses, such as touch, rely on nerve cells that send signals to your brain.

Your brain is the nervous system's control centre.

Other systems

Some of your other important systems are shown in this list.

Breathing system: the main organs are your lungs, which take in air.

Hormone system: this uses powerful chemicals to control your body and mood.

Skin, hair, and nails: these form your body's protective covering.

Immune system: this seeks and destroys germs that get into your body.

Urinary system: this cleans blood and gets rid of waste chemicals.

Reproductive system: these are the organs that make babies.

Digestive system

Your digestive organs break down food to provide your body with energy and raw materials.

Your mouth is the first part of the digestive system.

A long, twisting tube makes up your intestines, where digested food is absorbed.

The digestive system.

Bones and muscles

You would be like a lump of jelly without your skeleton – a frame of bones that holds you up and protects your internal organs.

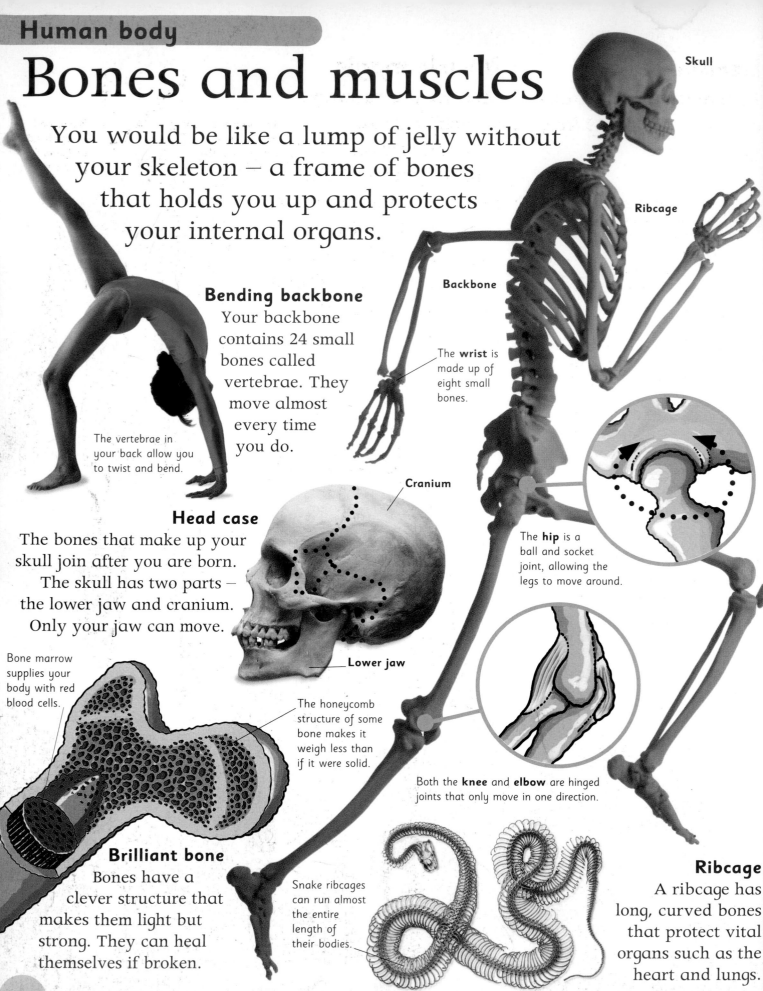

Skull

Ribcage

Backbone

Bending backbone
Your backbone contains 24 small bones called vertebrae. They move almost every time you do.

The vertebrae in your back allow you to twist and bend.

The **wrist** is made up of eight small bones.

Cranium

Head case
The bones that make up your skull join after you are born. The skull has two parts – the lower jaw and cranium. Only your jaw can move.

Lower jaw

The **hip** is a ball and socket joint, allowing the legs to move around.

Bone marrow supplies your body with red blood cells.

The honeycomb structure of some bone makes it weigh less than if it were solid.

Both the **knee** and **elbow** are hinged joints that only move in one direction.

Brilliant bone
Bones have a clever structure that makes them light but strong. They can heal themselves if broken.

Snake ribcages can run almost the entire length of their bodies.

Ribcage
A ribcage has long, curved bones that protect vital organs such as the heart and lungs.

How many bones does an adult human have?

Bending bits

Different kinds of joints all over your body keep you moving.

 Thumbs have joints that allow them to rotate, which fingers cannot do.

 Ankles contain different joints for up-and-down and side-to-side movement.

 Wrists have a joint that allows them to turn but not go all the way round.

 Neck bones feature a pivot joint that allows your head to turn.

Muscle magic

Muscles are rubbery, stretchy straps. You can control some of your muscles, like the muscles in your arms and legs. Others, such as your heart and bladder, operate without you having to think about it.

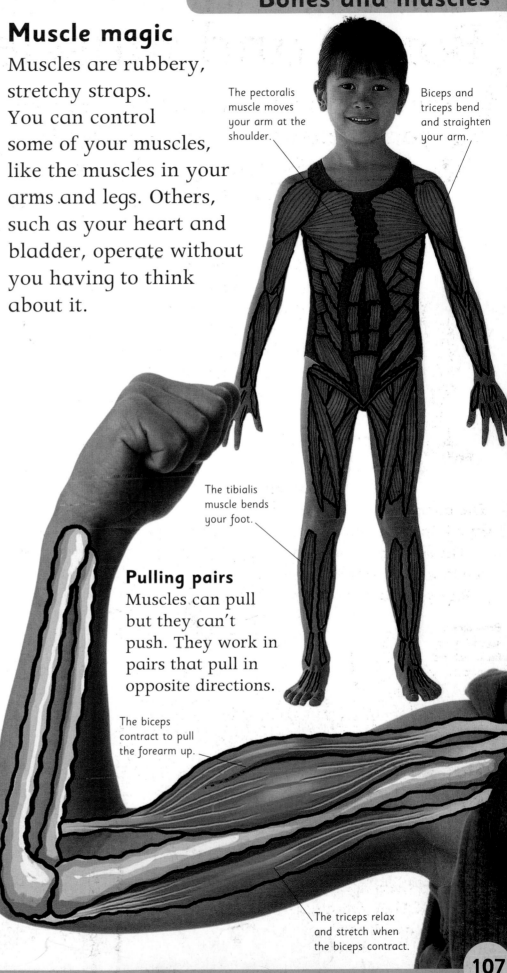

The pectoralis muscle moves your arm at the shoulder.

Biceps and triceps bend and straighten your arm.

The tibialis muscle bends your foot.

Making faces

Muscles in your face are attached to skin as well as bone. They allow you to make all kinds of expressions to show how you are feeling.

Pulling pairs

Muscles can pull but they can't push. They work in pairs that pull in opposite directions.

The biceps contract to pull the forearm up.

The triceps relax and stretch when the biceps contract.

You use your brain to think.

Brain and senses

Your brain is the part of your body that makes you think, feel, and remember. It makes sure that the rest of you works properly.

Different parts...

Your brain

Your brain is hidden inside your head. It looks a little bit like a soft, wrinkly lump of greyish-pink blancmange, or jelly.

Your hard, bony skull protects your brain from damage.

A bundle of nerves runs down your back, inside your backbone.

Nerves

Your brain is linked to your body by fibres called nerves. Nerves carry messages from your body to your brain, and back again.

Your brain weighs about the same as 12 apples.

If you prick your finger, your brain makes you feel pain.

Reflex actions

If you accidentally prick your finger on a rose thorn, your brain quickly makes you pull your hand away. This fast reaction is called a reflex action.

108

Do clever people have bigger brains?

Your senses

You know what is happening around you by seeing, hearing, smelling, tasting, and touching things. These are called your senses.

do different jobs.

Your eyes see the pictures, then your brain tells you what they are.

Eyes and seeing

Your eyes have special nerves that pick up light. They send messages to your brain, telling you what you are looking at.

Your ears pick up loud and soft sounds.

Ears and hearing

Your ears catch sounds and send them deep inside your head. Nerves send messages about the sounds to your brain.

Nose and smelling

Nerves inside your nose tell you what you are smelling. Some things, such as this rose, smell nice. Other things smell terrible!

Tongue and tasting

You taste with your tongue. It is covered with tiny bumps, called taste buds, which pick up tastes from your food.

Skin and touch

Nerves in your skin tell you if things feel hard, soft, hot, or cold. They also warn you of danger by making you feel pain.

Brown sugar   Grapes   Spaghetti

Can you tell what you are touching, without looking?

No. Everyone's brain is about the same size.

Breathing

We have to breathe all the time in order to supply our bodies with oxygen and to get rid of carbon dioxide. We use our lungs to do this.

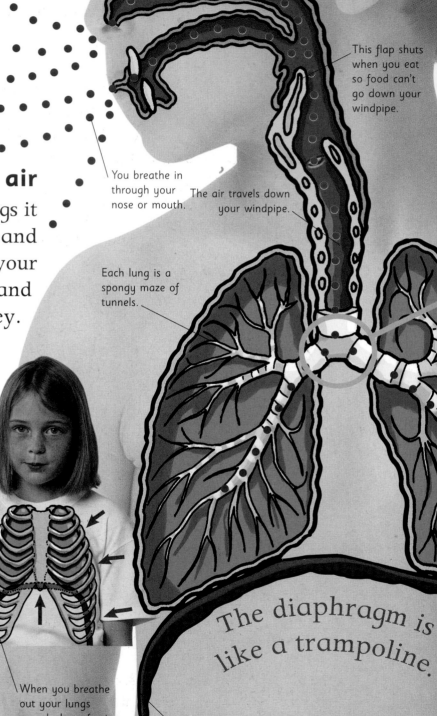

This flap shuts when you eat so food can't go down your windpipe.

You breathe in through your nose or mouth.

The air travels down your windpipe.

Each lung is a spongy maze of tunnels.

Prepare the air

Before the air reaches your lungs it travels through your mouth and nose and then goes down your windpipe. It gets warm and damp on its journey.

When you breathe in, your lungs stretch out and take in lots of air.

When you breathe out your lungs squash down forcing all the air out.

The diaphragm is like a trampoline.

The muscle under your lungs is called the diaphragm. It moves up and down as you breathe.

In and out

Your ribs and diaphragm help you to breathe. Your lungs fill with air when you raise your ribcage, then empty out when you lower it. A muscle called the diaphragm helps you do this.

110

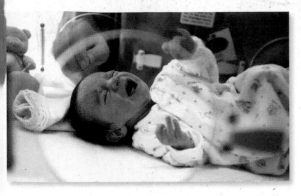

A helping hand

Some newborn babies have trouble breathing. They are put into an enclosed cradle called an incubator. Extra oxygen is pumped into the incubator for them.

The view from the bottom of your windpipe.

Windpipe

Air from your mouth and nose enters your windpipe, which goes down your throat into your chest. Then it splits into two passages – one for each lung.

The alveoli are surrounded by tiny blood capillaries to take the oxygen round the body.

Air sacs

Your lungs are full of tunnels ending in tiny air sacs called alveoli. Here, oxygen from the air passes into your blood. Your blood carries oxygen around every part of your body.

No lungs

Not every animal has lungs. There are other ways animals breathe.

Frogs can absorb oxygen through their skin – even underwater.

Insects such as caterpillars breathe through body openings called spiracles.

Many sea creatures such as sharks breathe through gills.

All about skin

Skin covers your whole body. It protects you from germs, water, and sunshine, and helps keep your body at the right temperature.

The skin on your eyelids is the thinnest on your body.

Two layers

Your skin has two main layers. The top one – the one you can see – is called the epidermis. Underneath is the dermis, where there are nerves and blood vessels.

Waterproof seal

Skin stops water getting into your body when you have a shower or go for a swim. It also stops fluids escaping from inside you.

There are flat cells on the surface of your skin. These are made from a tough material called keratin. When the cells die, they dry out and flake off.

Skin cells lower down replace the dead ones that flake off.

Skin is a sort of stretchy overcoat.

Magnified skin flakes

Heavy load

Skin is the heaviest single part of your body. It can weigh as much as a bag of shopping.

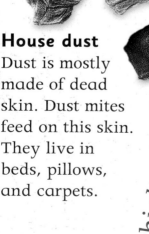

House dust

Dust is mostly made of dead skin. Dust mites feed on this skin. They live in beds, pillows, and carpets.

Dust mites aren't really this big! They're so small you can't see them.

The thickest skin on

How many dead-skin flakes fall off every day?

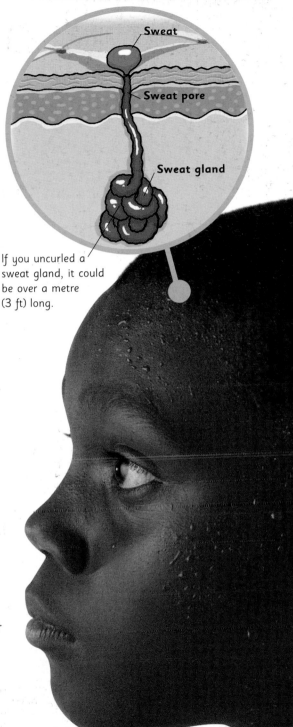

Sweat

Sweat pore

Sweat gland

If you uncurled a sweat gland, it could be over a metre (3 ft) long.

Skin colour

The colour of your skin is affected by a substance called melanin. The more melanin you have, the darker you will be. When you are outside in the sun, your body produces extra melanin to protect your skin. This melanin makes your skin darker and you get a suntan.

your body is on the soles of your feet.

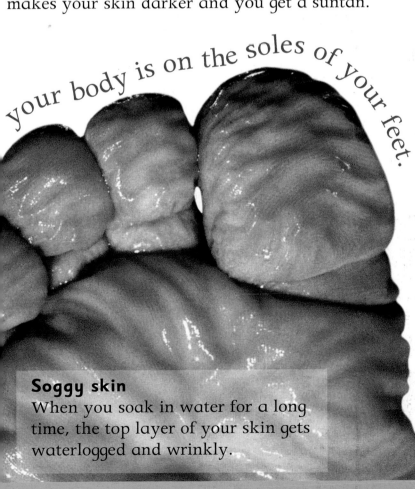

Soggy skin

When you soak in water for a long time, the top layer of your skin gets waterlogged and wrinkly.

Cooling down

When sweat dries on your skin, it helps to cool you down. Sweat comes from coiled tubes under the surface. It gets out through tiny holes called pores.

Body defences

Although you can't see them, germs are always landing on your body and trying to get inside it. Your body has lots of clever ways of keeping them out.

Poison tears

Germs that land on your eyes are washed away by tears, which come from glands above your eyes. Tears contain the chemical lysozyme, which kills bacteria by making them burst open.

You make about 1 litre (2 pints) of saliva a day.

Saved by spit

The liquid in your mouth is called saliva. As well as helping you digest food, saliva protects your mouth, tongue, and teeth from attack by bacteria.

Sticky business

Germs get into your lungs when you breathe in. They get trapped in a sticky liquid called mucus, which lines your airways. Tiny beating hairs continually push the mucus up to your throat to be swallowed.

Earwax flows slowly out of your ears all the time, flushing out dirt and germs.

Which is your largest defensive organ?

Acid attack

Glands inside your stomach make acid, which kills germs you've swallowed. Your digestive system then breaks down the germs along with your food.

Yuk!

The feeling of disgust protects you from germs. Anything that smells revolting or looks horrible is probably full of germs. Disgust stops you from touching it.

Slimy guts

The inside of your intestines are covered with slimy mucus, which stops germs from getting into your blood. Your large intestine also contains millions of "friendly" bacteria, which prevent other germs from growing.

Become an expert

110-111 Breathing
116-117 Eating and digestion

Eating and digestion

Your body needs food to keep it working. But before it can use the food, it breaks it into tiny pieces, which seep into your blood. This is called digestion.

Teeth
Tongue

Mouth

In your mouth, your teeth chop up and chew your food. Your spit helps to break food down and makes it easy to swallow. When you swallow, your food goes down a tube in your throat and into your stomach.

Your food travels through your body...

Become an expert

222-223 All living things
234-235 What is energy?

Stomach

Your stomach is like a stretchy bag that fills with food. Inside, your food is churned up and mixed with stomach juices. They break your food down into a thick soup-like mixture.

This tube diagram is not the same shape as the tubes inside your body.

This photograph of part of the stomach lining was taken through a microscope.

Why does your stomach rumble?

Intestines

Next, your food goes into long tubes called your intestines. It seeps through the walls of the intestines into your blood. Your blood takes the nutrients (goodness) in the food around your body.

Small intestine

This intestine is called your "small" intestine because it is narrow. In fact, it is as long as a bus!

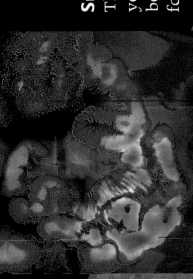

Intestine | Stomach

Your small and large intestines are coiled up inside your abdomen.

Small intestine

Large intestine

A meal takes one to three days to pass all the way through your digestive system.

Getting rid of waste

Any waste food travels from your small intestine into your large intestine. It is stored there until you go to the toilet and push it out as solid waste.

You get rid of waste water and solid waste when you go to the toilet.

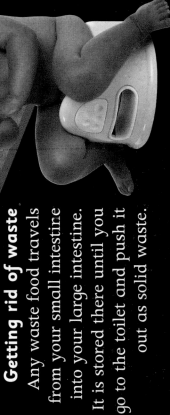

A balanced diet

You need to eat a mixture of foods to keep you strong and healthy. This is called a balanced diet.

Vitamins in fruit and vegetables keep your body working properly.

Fibre in wholemeal bread keeps your digestive system working.

Fat in butter and cheese gives you energy. Too much fat is bad for you.

Carbohydrates such as pasta, rice, and bread give you lots of energy.

Protein in milk helps you to grow and to repair your body.

...along a series of pipes and tubes.

Your mouth, stomach, and intestines are called your digestive system.

Because of air mixed up with your food.

Making a baby

You need a mother and a father to make a baby. The mother's body does most of the work, but the father also has an important job – his sperm joins with the mother's egg and a new life begins...

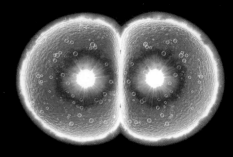

The first cells
After 36 hours, the cell has divided and made an exact copy of itself. These are the first two cells of a baby.

Eggs are the biggest cells in the human body. But they are still very small – ten would fit across a pinhead.

Sperm are amazing viewed under a microscope. They look like tiny tadpoles. You can see their tails wriggling as they swim.

Sperm race
Millions of sperm swim towards the egg cell. Only one sperm can join with the egg to make a new cell.

By the time the baby is born, the fertilized cell will have become 100 trillion cells.

What is another name for the uterus?

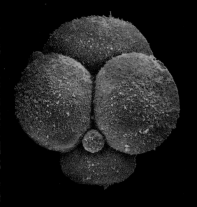

Divide again
You don't grow much in the first few days. The two cells divide to make four, then eight, and so on.

The future you
Each cell is unique to you. Cells are full of instructions about what you will look like.

At three days
The cells have carried on dividing. There are now 16 cells and they are almost ready to plant themselves in the uterus.

Where it all happens
The sperm fertilizes the egg in a tunnel, called a fallopian tube. The fertilized egg moves down the tunnel towards the mother's uterus. The journey takes about five days.

The cells start dividing as they move down the fallopian tube towards the uterus.

Millions of sperm from the father travel up here towards the egg.

This is the mother's ovary. It releases one egg every month.

This is the uterus. It is about the size of a pear and has muscular walls.

Arriving in the uterus
The ball of cells plants itself in the wall of the uterus. In this warm, dark place the baby will spend the next 40 weeks growing and developing.

Amazing facts about YOU!

Skeleton and bones

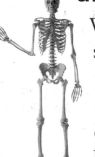

Without a skeleton to hold you up, you'd collapse on the ground like a heap of jelly.

Your smallest bone is the stapes in your ear, which is smaller than a rice grain.

Weight for weight, bones are stronger than steel or concrete.

A baby has more than 300 bones but adults have only 206.

Muscles and movement

Muscles move your body by pulling bones. You use hundreds of them when you walk.

Every hair in your body has a tiny muscle that can pull it upright.

Your strongest muscle is the masseter (jaw muscle), which closes your mouth.

You use more muscles when you frown than when you smile.

Brain and nerves

Your brain is the body's control centre. Signals zoom to and from the brain along your nerves.

Nerves carry signals at up to 400 kph (250 mph).

Your brain is made of about 100 billion tiny cells called neurons.

The left side of your brain controls the right side of your body and vice versa.

The human eye can see a candle flame at night from 1.6 km (1 mile) away.

When you're bored, the pupils in your eyes get smaller.

Heart and blood

Your heart pumps blood around your body. It works nonstop without getting tired.

Your smallest blood vessels are ten times thinner than a hair.

Your body contains enough blood vessels to circle the world twice.

Breathing

Lungs take air into your body so that life-giving oxygen can enter your blood.

The inside of your lungs is as big as a third of a tennis court.

The fastest recorded sneeze reached 167 kph (104 mph).

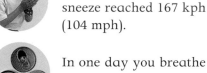
In one day you breathe in enough air to fill 33,000 drink cans.

Skin, nails, and hair

The tough, protective surface of your body is almost entirely dead.

Every four years you shed your own body weight in dead skin.

You have about 5 million hairs, but only 100,000 are on your head.

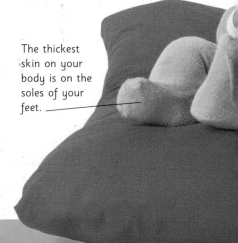
The thickest skin on your body is on the soles of your feet.

Fighting disease

Germs are always trying to get inside you, but your body fights back.

 Many germs are not harmful, but some cause illness, and even death.

 Bacteria are so small that a thousand could fit on the head of a pin.

 The world's most common disease is the common cold.

 Cancer happens when your own cells multiply out of control.

 When you recover from an infectious disease, your body becomes immune to it.

Digestive system

Digestion turns food into simple chemicals that your body can make into new cells or use for fuel.

 The food you eat in a year weighs as much as a car.

 You make enough spit in your lifetime to fill two swimming pools.

 Your digestive glands start working as soon as you smell or see food.

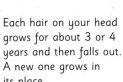 Your tongue senses five tastes: salty, sweet, sour, bitter, and savoury.

 The smell of poo comes from a chemical called skatole.

Each hair on your head grows for about 3 or 4 years and then falls out. A new one grows in its place.

Urinary system

Urine gets rid of chemicals that your body doesn't need.

 You will make enough urine in your lifetime to fill 500 baths.

 Asparagus can turn your urine green. Blackberries can turn it red.

Reproduction

The reproductive organs create new people from tiny specks of matter.

 The most babies born to one mother was 69. Most were twins, triplets, or quads.

 The first quintuplets known to have survived infancy were born in 1934.

Growth

As you grow you slowly change into an adult, but it takes a long time!

 The fastest-growing part of a baby's body is its head.

 A girl is about three-quarters of her adult height at 7 years old.

 A boy is about three-quarters of his adult height at 9 years old.

The living world

Our amazing world is filled with millions of species, or types, of living thing. They can be as big as an elephant or so small you have to look through a microscope to see them.

Spider

Dragonfly

Animals

The animal kingdom is made up of vertebrates (animals with a backbone) and invertebrates (animals without a backbone).

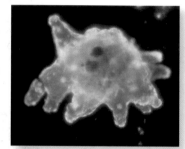

Micro-organisms

Micro-organisms are very tiny – they are made up of a single cell. This amoeba is magnified more than 100 times.

Coral reef

Mammals, birds, reptiles, amphibians, and fish are vertebrates.

Deer

Sunflower

122

Snake

Insects such as butterflies are invertebrates.

Plants

Plants cannot move around like animals. To survive and grow, they have to make their own food. In turn, plants provide food for many animals and fungi.

Signs of life

Living things share some characteristics. They all need food and oxygen. They also grow, reproduce, and adapt to their environment.

Fungi

Tree frog

Fungi (like toadstools, mushrooms, and moulds) are neither plants nor animals, but they're more like plants than animals.

Fungi

Curiosity quiz

Look through The living world pages and see if you can identify the pictures below.

Become an expert

126-127 Types of animals

148-149 How plants work

Invertebrates – they make up 97 per cent of all animal species.

What is an animal?

A key definition of an animal, as opposed to a plant, is that most animals can move voluntarily. Animals must also eat other living things to survive. Let's take a look at some of the things animals do.

Bald eagle

Food is fuel

All animals have to find and eat food to survive. Carnivores are animals that eat meat. Herbivores eat mainly plants. Omnivores are creatures that eat both plants and meat.

Squirrels eat seeds, nuts, fruit, and fungi.

Getting around

Many animals have muscles, which allow them to move in a variety of ways.

 Flying: birds fly by flapping wings or gliding on currents of hot air.

 Swimming: animals like fish swim by moving their bodies and fins.

 Slithering: some snakes wriggle, others raise and flatten their bodies.

 Walking and running: many animals walk and run using legs.

 Reaching: sea anemones reach out their tentacles to sting prey.

What a nerve!

Animals have nerves, which carry information from their sense organs. Most animals have brains to monitor this information. The nerves also carry orders from the brain to the organs and muscles – such as instructions to stay still, attack, or run away!

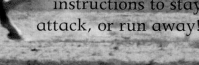

How many species of animal are there on Earth?

Do animals talk?
Many animals are able to communicate with each other.

Most beetles will send "messages" to other beetles using special chemicals.

Pythons can go without food for months after one BIG meal!

Making babies

Most animals reproduce when a female egg is fertilized by a male sperm. Some animals give birth to babies, while others lay eggs.

Birds lay hard-shelled eggs, which hatch into chicks or ducklings.

Baby birds have to break out of the egg on their own.

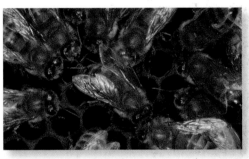

Honey bees communicate constantly. They give directions with a special dance.

Giraffes have seven vertebrae in their neck – the same as most other mammals. They are just much longer.

Monkeys scream at each other to sound an alarm.

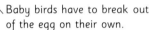

Nobody knows the exact answer, but about 1.8 million have been identified.

Types of animals

There are so many different types, or species, of animals that scientists put them in groups so it's easier to study them. Mammals, birds, reptiles, amphibians, and fish are vertebrates. Creepy-crawlies are invertebrates.

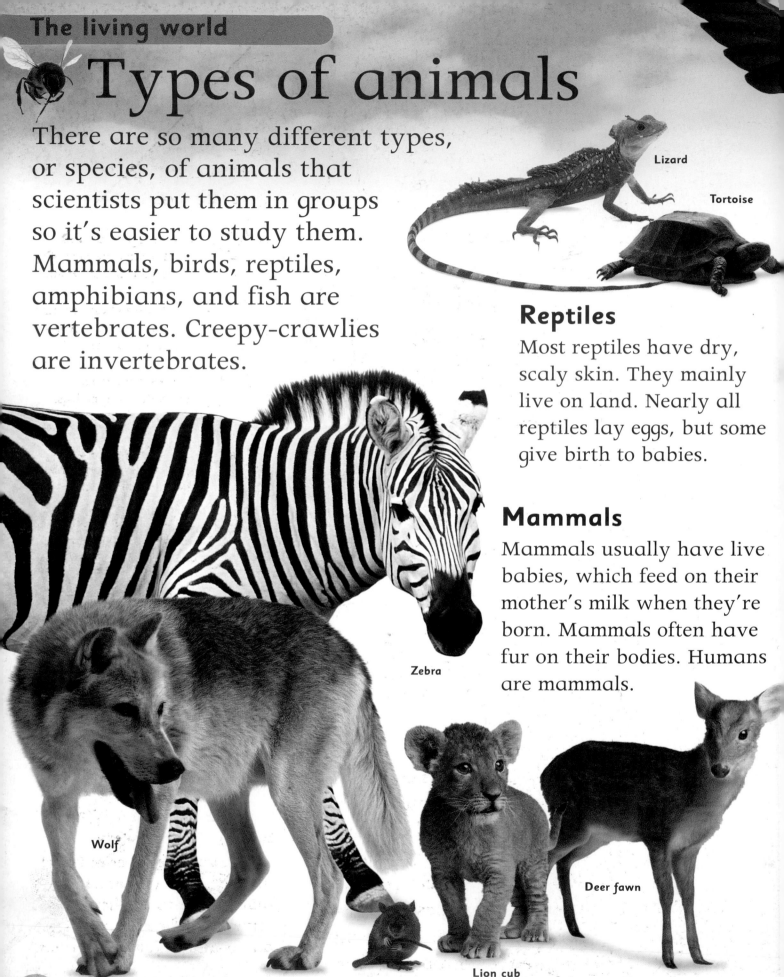

Lizard

Tortoise

Reptiles

Most reptiles have dry, scaly skin. They mainly live on land. Nearly all reptiles lay eggs, but some give birth to babies.

Mammals

Mammals usually have live babies, which feed on their mother's milk when they're born. Mammals often have fur on their bodies. Humans are mammals.

Zebra

Wolf

Deer fawn

Mouse

Lion cub

What is the only mammal that can fly?

Birds

All birds have wings, and most (but not all) can fly. They have feathers and a beak. Baby birds hatch from eggs.

Parrot

Ostriches can run fast but can't fly.

Amphibians

Amphibians live both in water and on land. They usually have slimy skin. Baby amphibians hatch from jelly-like eggs.

Frog

Salamander

Fish

Fish need to live in water. They breathe through gills, and most are covered in scales. Fish use their fins to move through water.

Spineless creatures

Animals without backbones are called invertebrates. There are several types of invertebrates.

 Insects, spiders, and crustaceans are part of the largest animal group.

 Snails and slugs are part of an invertebrate group called gastropods.

Worms have long, soft bodies and no legs. They like damp areas.

 Jellyfish, starfish, and sponges are invertebrates that live in water.

 Octopus and squid live in the sea. They have eight arms.

Butterfly

Ladybird

Insects

There are more types of insect on Earth than any other animal. Insects can live almost anywhere. They have six legs and bodies with three sections.

The bat.

127

The world of mammals

Mammals include animals such as the whale, the kangaroo, and you and me! We all have fur, we are warm blooded, and we feed new babies with our milk.

Gorilla
skeleton

Mammal babies

Most mammal females give birth to live babies, rather than laying eggs. The baby grows inside the mother's body until it is born.

The skeleton

Mammals may look very different, but stripped back to the bone we all have the basic bony skeleton. Scientists call us vertebrates – animals with a backbone.

Feeding babies

All female mammals produce milk from their bodies that they feed to their babies; this feeding is called suckling. The milk is rich and helps the babies to grow.

Become an expert

130-131 Marsupials
132-133 Water mammals

This baby gorilla is a member of the primate family.

Within the mammal group there are many different families.

Baby gorilla

128

Polar bears can live in chilly Arctic regions because they are warm blooded and have thick fur.

Hairy beasts

All mammals are hairy – some are much hairier than others – and most have hair, often called fur, all over their bodies. They are hairy to keep them warm.

Elephant

This elephant may not look hairy but it does have hair on its body.

Warm blood

Mammals are warm blooded, which means they can warm up and cool down their bodies to keep their temperature level. An elephant in the hot jungle is the same temperature as a polar bear in the snow.

Polar bear

Getting around

Mammals are many different shapes that suit their lifestyles.

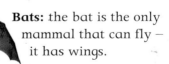

Cats: some mammals, such as the cat, have long legs to run with.

Bats: the bat is the only mammal that can fly – it has wings.

Dolphins: sea mammals have flippers and strong tails to swim with.

Moles: the mole has feet like spades, which are useful for burrowing.

The polar bear has thick fur all over its body.

The odd one out

It is usually true that animals give birth to live babies, but there are a few species, including this duck-billed platypus, that lay eggs. Platypus eggs are soft and the size of marbles.

129

There are about 4,500 different types of mammal in the world.

Marsupials

A marsupial is a mammal with a pocket called a pouch for carrying its babies in.

Koala

Koalas look like little bears. They live in Australia and are the only animal that eats eucalyptus leaves. They are so hard to digest that koalas spend 19 hours of the day sleeping to let their tummies settle.

When the baby koala gets too big for the pouch, it clings to its mother's back instead.

More marsupials

Apart from a few that live in South America, almost all marsupials come from Australasia. They vary a lot in looks.

Dorian's tree kangaroo: this small kangaroo can climb trees.

Numbat: this marsupial has the most teeth of any mammal. It has 52.

Rabbit-eared bandicoot: is a burrower with big ears.

Little devil

The Tasmanian devil is not much bigger than a small dog but is very aggressive. It is the biggest meat-eating marsupial and has such powerful jaws that it can eat an entire animal – bones and all!

A kangaroo's front legs are

Bouncing marsupials

Kangaroos cannot walk. Instead they have enormous back legs that they use to jump everywhere. They can move very fast just by leaping.

Become an expert

Which are bigger, wallabies or kangaroos?

Opossums are very good tree climbers.

Supermum!

Opossums live in the Americas. Unusually for marsupials, the mother has no pouch. Instead her babies cling to her. Sometimes one mother can have up to 20 babies at one time!

This joey is definitely big enough to climb out of its pouch.

In the pouch

Most marsupials have pouches. When the babies are born, they are as small as beans and wriggle straight into the pouch. They do most of their growing there, instead of in their mother's tummy.

Little joey

Kangaroo and wallaby babies are commonly known as joeys. They spend several months in the mother's pouch, and even when they are big enough to walk, they sometimes jump back in for safety.

not used when they bounce

Their huge tails help to balance them when they run.

Kangaroos look like wallabies, but they are bigger.

Water mammals

Not all mammals live on land – some live in water. Unlike fish, however, water mammals have to go to the surface to breathe.

Seals

Seals, which include sea lions and walruses, have flippers instead of arms and legs, which make them very good at swimming but not good at walking.

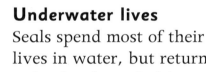

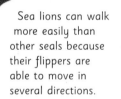

Sea lions can walk more easily than other seals because their flippers are able to move in several directions.

Sea lion

Underwater lives

Seals spend most of their lives in water, but return to land to have babies. They have a thick layer of fat, called blubber, which keeps them warm.

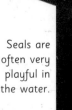

Seals are often very playful in the water.

What noise do seals make?

Otters

Otters are small mammals that have webbed feet to help them swim. The river otter lives along river banks and spends its day swimming to catch food.

Otters of the sea

The sea otter is the smallest sea mammal. It has luxurious, thick fur that keeps it very warm. It rarely comes to land, and even sleeps in the water. When it nods off, it wraps itself up in kelp plants to stop it from drifting away!

Sea cows

Manatees are often called sea cows because they are so big and they "graze", like cows, on river-bed plants. They spend all their lives underwater, and even give birth there.

Walruses

Walruses are huge sea mammals that have massive, blubbery bodies and very wrinkly skin. They heave themselves out of the water to rest and breed.

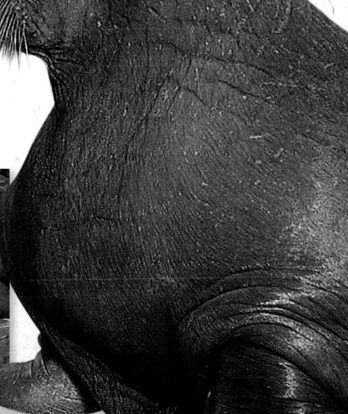

Walruses use their noses, like pigs, to root around the sea floor for food, such as crabs or sea urchins.

Walrus

In the pink

Walruses are normally greyish-brown in colour. But when they sunbathe, they blush pink because their blood rushes to the surface of their skin to cool them.

Seals bark like dogs!

The world of birds

Only a few animals in the world are able to fly – insects, bats, and birds. But none of them is more powerful or skilled than the bird.

Birds spend much of their time looking after, or preening, their feathers to keep them in good condition.

Feathers are made up of tiny hair-like barbs that all mesh together.

Feathered friends

Birds are the only creatures that have feathers. They use them to fly and to keep warm. Some birds use brightly coloured feathers for display.

A rigid "backbone" or quill runs through the centre of the wing feathers to strengthen them for flying.

Feathers

Different feathers have different jobs on a bird.

Outer wing: strong feathers to provide power in flight.

Inner wing: smooth and flat to help flight.

Tail feather: long and thin for steering and balancing during flight.

Body feather: soft and downy to keep a bird warm. Some have exotic colours.

Birds' feet are designed for different purposes, such as climbing, clutching berries, or holding on to branches.

What is the world's smallest bird?

Flight

A bird can fly because it has wings and a very light skeleton – many of the bones are hollow. Birds have short and compact bodies that make them neat fliers too.

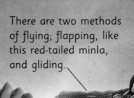
There are two methods of flying; flapping, like this red-tailed minla, and gliding.

Red-tailed minla

By flapping its wings up and down, the bird remains in the air.

Travelling birds

About one-third of birds spend summer in one place then when the winter sets in they fly thousands of miles to a warmer spot. Often they go to exactly the same places year after year.

Feet

The shape of birds' feet vary depending on where they live.

Eagle foot: birds of prey have sharp talons to kill and grip animals.

Perching foot: songbirds have three toes in front and one behind for perching.

Webbed foot: waterfowl have webbed feet to help them to paddle on water.

Ostrich foot: two thick toes help this flightless bird to run very fast.

Bills

The shape and size of a bird's bill, or beak, can show what they eat.

Duck: wide and flat to tear plants and filter food underwater.

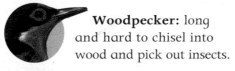
Woodpecker: long and hard to chisel into wood and pick out insects.

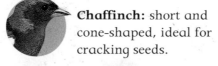
Chaffinch: short and cone-shaped, ideal for cracking seeds.

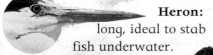
Heron: long, ideal to stab fish underwater.

Communication

All birds have good hearing so they can respond to songs from other members of their family. Birds are well known for their tunes, and some, like this parrot, even speak.

The world of reptiles

Reptiles are egg-laying animals that have a tough skin covered in scales. They live on land and in water.

The reptile groups

There are four main groups of reptiles:

The tortoise family: these reptiles all have a shell over their body.

Snakes and lizards: the majority of reptiles fall into this group.

The crocodile family: this group are the giants of the reptile world.

Tuataras: these reptiles are very rare and look a bit like lizards.

Reptiles can eat huge meals, then go without food for days.

Most reptiles, swing their bodies from side to side when walking.

Eating habits

Reptiles are meat eaters, with the exception of tortoises, which move too slowly to catch fast-moving prey. Lizards, such as this gecko, can eat half their own weight in insects in one night.

All reptiles shed their skin from time to time.

Flying gecko

Hot and cold

Reptiles have scales, which can control how much water they lose through their skin. This means they can live in dry places. They are cold blooded, however, so rely on the climate to keep their temperature in check.

European eyed lizard

Reptile babies

Nearly all reptiles lay eggs, which hatch into miniature versions of their parents. A few, such as this slow worm, however, give birth to live young.

This lizard, which lives in the deser basks on rocks to warm up its boc

What is the longest snake in the world?

Tuataras live in burrows and hunt at night. They can live for 100 years.

Living fossils

Tuataras are the only survivors of a group of reptiles that lived with the dinosaurs millions of years ago. Today they live on a group of islands off New Zealand.

Scaly skin

A reptile's skin is covered with scales made of keratin, like your nails.

Tortoise: the shell of a tortoise has lots of large, hard scales on it.

Lizard: Lizards' scales have stretchy skin between them.

Crocodile: these scales are strengthened in between by bony plates.

Snake: the skin on snakes has overlapping scales for extra protection.

Reptile relatives

The reptiles of today are the last living relatives of dinosaurs and look very similar to their ancient ancestors. You can see similarities between the *Tyrannosaurus rex* and this lizard.

Tyrannosaurus rex

Collared lizard

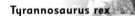

Become an expert

138-139 The world of amphibians
144-145 The world of fish

The reticulated python can reach lengths of 10 m (33 ft).

The world of amphibians

Amphibians are different from reptiles in that they have smooth skin with no scales. They are born in water then live on land or in water when they grow up.

Fire salamander

Amazing skin

Most adult amphibians, such as this salamander, can breathe through their skin as well as their lungs. In order for the skin to breathe it has to be kept moist, which is why most amphibians like to live near water.

Some frogs live in water...

Amphibian family

There are three groups in the amphibian family.

Frogs and toads: these amphibians have no tail and big back legs.

Newts and salamanders: these lizard-shaped animals live on land or in water.

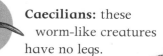

Caecilians: these worm-like creatures have no legs.

Frog

Become an expert

142-143 The world of non-insects
144-145 The world of fish

Colourful creatures

Many amphibians are incredibly colourful creatures. Some are spotted, others are striped and some are just very bright.

What is the world's most poisonous frog?

A choice of home

Frogs and toads can
live both on land
and in water.
Some even
live in trees.

Land frogs tend to
be more rounded
in shape than
water frogs.

Water living

Some salamanders
spend the whole of
their lives underwater.
This cave salamander does not
have any lungs; it breathes through its
skin only. It is almost completely blind.

...other frogs prefer to live in the tops of tall trees!

Caecilians

Legless caecilians are rarely seen by
humans because they live either under
water or under ground. They have a
pointed head, which they use as a shovel.

If an animal is poisonous like this tomato frog, it
is often a very bright colour that warns predators.

Travelling parents

Each spring salamanders,
newts, frogs, and toads
lay their eggs in ponds
or streams. Some travel
5 km (3 miles) to get there.

Common
newt

The most poisonous frog is the bright-yellow poison-dart frog.

The world of insects

A huge majority of creepy crawlies are insects. In fact there are more types of insect in the world than any other animal. They are absolutely everywhere. Some are almost too small to see and others are surprisingly large.

Remember, insects have 3 + 3. Three pairs of legs and three body parts.

Most insects have two pairs of wings.

Beetle

When a pile of dung appears in Africa, dung beetles are on the scene in minutes.

The beetles roll perfect balls of dung in which they lay a single egg. When the egg hatches, the larva eats the dung.

What is an insect?

You can tell if a creepy crawly is an insect because insects always have six legs. They also have three body parts – a head, a thorax, and an abdomen.

Nature's recycling service

Although many people dislike insects and they can be pests, they are also essential to our world. In fact we could not live without them. For instance, these dung beetles do a very good job cleaning up dung.

Dung beetles

Apart from honey, what else does a bee produce that we can use?

Useful insects

Here are some other ways that insects are useful to us.

Red food dye: this food colouring is made from the bodies of scale insects.

Silk: believe it or not, the silk you wear is made by silk-moth caterpillars!

Honey: if there were no bees in the world, we would have no honey.

Food: to some people, such as the Australian aborigines, grubs are a meal.

As old as an insect

We know that insects were around 40 million years ago because some were trapped in a tree resin called amber, which hardened back then and preserved them.

Pest control

Sometimes insects, such as aphids, eat huge amounts of our crops. The best way to get rid of them is to introduce another insect that likes to eat them. Ladybirds are often used for aphid pest control.

Aphid

Introducing insects that eat other insects is called biological pest control.

Ladybird

Aphids breed so quickly that it is difficult to control them.

Become an expert

Bees produce wax and their poison is used as medicine.

The world of non-insects

There are many creepy crawlies scuttling around our planet that are not insects. Some live on land, others live in fresh water or the sea. They come in all sorts of weird and wonderful shapes.

Arachnids

Spiders, scorpions, ticks, and mites belong to a land-dwelling family called arachnids. All arachnids have eight legs and two body parts.

Tarantula

The worm family
Segmented worms like earthworms are simple animals that have a head at one end, a tail at the other, and lots of segmented body parts in between. They live on land or in water.

Despite their reputation, most spiders are harmless to humans.

A tarantula has hairs on its legs that can cause bad irritation. When the spider is annoyed, it flicks them out at the enemy.

How big can spiders grow?

Odd sea creatures

The sea contains some very strange animals indeed. Here are a few:

Sponge: these animals were once thought to be plants.

Starfish: most starfish have five arms to crawl across the sea floor.

Anemone: these flower-like sea animals have no brains.

Snail

Snails are found on land and in the sea.

Molluscs

Slugs, snails, squids, and oysters, are molluscs. Some live on land and some live in water.

The octopus, which is also a mollusc, is a very intelligent creature.

Centipede

Centipede

Millipede

Centipedes have one pair of legs on each segment and millipedes have two pairs on each.

Centipedes and millipedes

If you try counting the legs on an insect and you find there are too many, the chances are you have found a centipede or millipede. They have lots and lots of legs.

Crustaceans

Most crustaceans, such as lobsters, crabs, and shrimps, live in water. Only the woodlouse lives on land. They often have a shell and their eyes are on stalks.

Lobster

Some spiders can grow as big as dinner plates!

The world of fish

Fish have been around for 400 million years! They live in seas, rivers, and lakes. Wherever you find water, you can bet there are plenty of fish swimming around.

Types of fish

There are over 24,000 types of fish, which fall into three groups.

Bony fish: 95% of the fish in the world are bony fish with hard skeletons.

Cartilaginous fish: rays, skates, and sharks make up this group.

Jawless fish: only hagfish and lampreys fall into this small group.

Bony fish have a skeleton with a skull, ribs, and a backbone.

Pyjama cardinalfish

Fish skin, made up of scales, is slimy to let them slip through water easily.

The gills lie behind the eyes.

Fish have fins that keep them upright when they swim.

The tail of a fish sweeps from side to side to push the fish forwards.

Gills

Like other animals, fish need to take in oxygen in order to live. But, unlike us, they can breathe underwater using their gills. Fish gulp in water and their gills filter the oxygen out of it.

Fish out of water

Mudskippers are one of the only fish that can survive out of water. They have special gills that take oxygen from air or water. They skip along mudflats using their fins as elbows.

Mudskipper

144

Which fish is the slowcoach of the sea?

The art of swimming

Many fish swim like snakes slide – they wriggle in an 's' shape. Their whole bodies move from side to side and their tails flick to push them forwards. Their fins help to steer them.

Scales

Most fish are covered in hundreds of scales that overlap like roof tiles. Tiny animals can get under the scales and harm them, so fish let other creatures give them a regular clean.

Colours can be used for camouflage or to attract a mate.

Mandarin fish

Carp

Some fish can turn on their sides and roll right over. A few can even swim upside-down!

Colour

Fish come in all colours and patterns. Freshwater fish and those living in cooler waters tend to be duller in colour. Tropical fish are sometimes incredibly bright and beautiful.

Eels are found in fresh water and sea water.

Living together

Fish sometimes swim in huge groups called schools. When so many swim together they look like one big fish so they are less likely to be attacked.

Fishy features

Most fish look like the pyjama cardinalfish on the left. Some however have a different appearance. This eel looks more like a snake with fins. Unlike a snake it has sharp teeth.

The seahorse is the slowest fish that lives in the sea.

What is a plant?

Plants make their own food from the Sun's rays. Most have leaves that reach outwards to capture sunlight, and roots that dig deep for nutrients and stability.

Plant parts

There are loads of different plants, but most are made of the same vital parts – roots, stems, leaves, and flowers.

Stems

Stems support the leaves and flowers and allow water and food to flow from the roots to the leaves.

Roots

These are the foundations of the plant. They dig deep into the dirt giving stability, as well as sucking up nutrients.

Seaweed

Seaweed looks like a plant, but is an algae. It doesn't have roots, so it has to stick to rocks or float with the tide.

The petals attract insects and birds that collect pollen.

The stamen and carpels form the reproductive organs of a plant.

Flowers

Flowers are key to plant reproduction. They make pollen and develop seeds and fruit.

Leaves

These are the work factories of the plant and capture the Sun's energy.

Water lily

The water lily's flat leaves float on the pond surface, as its roots sink into the pond bed.

weird or what?

The Venus flytrap doesn't just get its energy from the Sun. It also lures and feeds on unsuspecting insects. Yum!

What plant has the largest leaves?

Types of plants

Have a look around you. Not all plants are the same. But some plants are more similar than others.

Fern leaves unfurl as they grow.

Ferns

Ferns love damp and shady areas. They have prong-like leaves and spread using spores.

Most conifer trees keep their leaves all year round.

Moss

Mosses love moisture and grow in clumps. They don't have roots or grow flowers.

There are about 12,000 species of moss.

Conifers

Conifer trees grow cones that store their seeds. Most conifers have needle-shaped leaves.

The sequoia is the largest tree in the world.

You can identify a tree by the shape of its leaves.

Ash leaf

Maple leaf

Scarlet oak leaf

Flowering plants

This is the biggest group of plants. They produce flowers, fruits and seeds, which mainly grow in seasonal cycles.

Rainforest

These warm and wet forests are home to nearly half the world's plant species.

Deciduous

Deciduous plants shed their leaves to save food and survive drier seasons.

Ash leaf

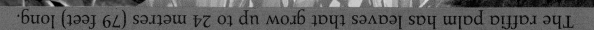

The raffia palm has leaves that grow up to 24 metres (79 feet) long.

How plants work

Plants have an amazing system for making and transporting food to all their different parts.

Photosynthesis

The green pigment chlorophyll traps sunlight in the leaves. The Sun's energy is then used to change water and carbon dioxide into sugar.

The Sun's energy is trapped in the leaves, and helps make food.

Cross-section through a leaf vein

Food is moved from leaves to roots and growing tips, along a set of tubes called phloem vessels.

A waste product of photosynthesis is oxygen, which animals need to survive.

Some water evaporates through tiny holes called stomata in the surface of the leaf. This process is called transpiration.

Tiny tubes called xylem vessels carry water up the stem from the roots to the leaves.

Cross-section through a stem

Veins carry water around the leaf.

Roots suck water up from the ground.

Are plants the only organism to use photosynthesis?

New growth

Plants use sugar and starch as fuel. The fuel is transported to cells where it is burnt to release energy, which is used to grow new cells and repair old ones.

Wilting leaves

On warm, sunny days, plants lose lots of water from their leaves. If they lose too much their leaves collapse. This is called wilting. If plants don't get enough water their leaves will shrivel and die.

Desert plants

Plants that live in dry areas such as deserts have to save their water. Many have leaves that are thick and covered in wax to stop transpiration. Cacti have spines rather than leaves and thick stems in which they can store water.

Fruit acts as a store of sugar and water.

Carrot plants store food in their roots.

Bulb

Storing food

Spare food is stored for future use. Plants such as hyacinths store food in the base of their leaves. This makes the leaves swell and form a bulb. The bulb survives the winter and in spring it sprouts new leaves.

Hands on

Place a stem of celery in a glass of water coloured with a few drops of food colouring. After two hours, cut across the stem. You will see tiny dots of colour showing the tubes that carry the water.

No, many bacteria also make food by photosynthesis.

Fungi

Mushrooms, toadstools, yeasts, and moulds are all kinds of fungi. Fungi are neither animals nor plants. They feed on living or dead animals or plants, and absorb their nutrients.

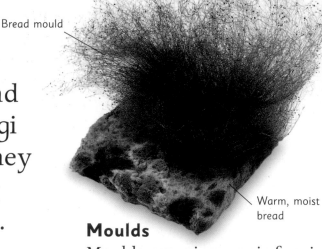

Bread mould

Warm, moist bread

Moulds

Moulds are microscopic fungi which grow in long strands called "hyphae". They feed on dead organic matter – like our food – by making it rot.

Mushrooms

Many fungi are hidden in the soil, or inside food sources like trees. They only become visible when they grow mushrooms. Mushrooms scatter spores, which will grow into new fungi.

Gills

Stem

The gills release spores into the air.

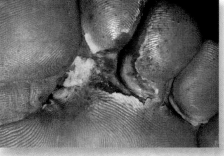

Athlete's foot

Athlete's foot is a disease caused by ringworm fungi growing on human feet. It makes the skin between your toes turn red and flaky.

Picking wild mushrooms

Many wild mushrooms are not only edible, but delicious. However others are highly poisonous! Harmful mushrooms are often called toadstools. They sometimes use bright colours to warn animals not to eat them.

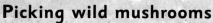

Wood blewit mushroom

Penny bun mushroom

Fly agaric mushroom

Jelly antler fungus

How big is the world's largest fungus?

Penicillin

In 1928, Sir Alexander Fleming made an important discovery. He realised that the mould *Penicillium notatum* makes a chemical that kills bacteria. That chemical, called penicillin, is used today as a medicine to treat many illnesses.

Sir Alexander Fleming (1881–1955)

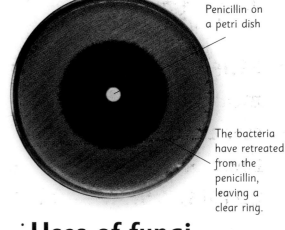

Penicillin on a petri dish

The bacteria have retreated from the penicillin, leaving a clear ring.

Truffles

Truffles are strong-smelling fungi that grow underground. They are a delicacy used in cookery. Truffle hunters use pigs and dogs to sniff them out.

White truffle

Black perigord truffle

Yeast

Yeast are microscopic, single-celled fungi. When they feed, they turn sugar into carbon-dioxide gas and alcohol. Yeast plays an important part in bread-making. As it releases gas, it makes bread rise.

Uses of fungi

Fungi have many uses in the home and in industry.

Medicine: Fungi can be used to cure many diseases that were once fatal.

Wine: Yeast turns grape juice into wine by changing sugar into alcohol.

Cheese: Blue cheeses are made with a mould called *Penicillium roquefortii*.

Soy sauce: This is made by adding fungi and yeast to soy beans and roasted wheat.

Pesticide: Fungi can be an environmentally friendly way of killing insects or weeds.

Shaggy parasol mushroom

Shaggy cap mushroom

Common chantarelle mushroom

Chicken of the woods fungus

A mushroom under the Malheur National Forest, USA, covers 8.9 square kilometres.

Micro life

Most living things are made up of just one cell, and are too small to see. To study them we must use powerful microscopes.

Bacteria

Bacteria are single-celled life forms. They are found in the ocean, in the air, and even in our bodies. They can reproduce very quickly by splitting in two. Some bacteria can make energy from sunlight. However, most feed on dead plants and animals.

Harmful bacteria

Some bacteria can cause serious illnesses such as cholera and tetanus. Good sanitation and antibiotic drugs help fight diseases caused by harmful bacteria.

Bacteria may be shaped like rods, spirals, or spheres.

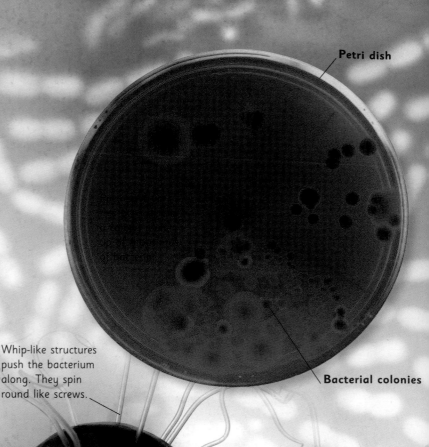

Petri dish

Bacterial colonies

Whip-like structures push the bacterium along. They spin round like screws.

Model of a bacterium

Thin hairs attach the bacterium to a surface.

The cell is full of a jelly-like substance that helps it to work and grow.

The bacterium's DNA code is held in the nucleus.

The cell wall holds the bacterium together and protects it.

Good bacteria

Some bacteria are helpful to humans. Bacteria in our guts protect us from illnesses. Other bacteria are used to make foods such as yoghurt and cheese.

152

How many copies can a single bacterium make of itself in 24 hours?

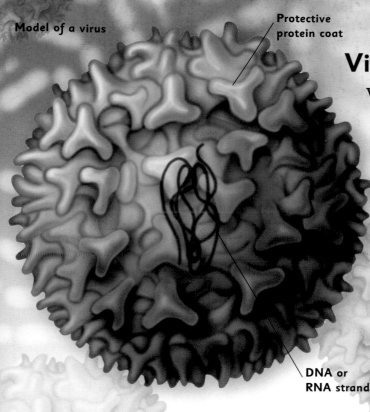

Model of a virus

Protective protein coat

DNA or RNA strand

Viruses

Viruses are many times smaller than bacteria. They are shaped like spheres or rods. Viruses are not really alive, because they are not made of cells. They only become active when they invade a cell. They copy themselves by taking over the cell and turning it into a virus factory.

Plant viruses

Plant viruses can change the way that plants develop. For example, one virus affects the pigment in tulips' petals. It stops the pigment from working in some places. This makes the petals look stripey.

Vaccinations

Vaccinations can help to protect people from harmful diseases. A person is injected with a weakened form of a virus or bacterium. This helps the immune system defend itself against the real thing.

A virus has made light patches appear on these leaves.

The streaked patterns on this tulip are caused by a virus.

Harmful viruses

Viruses can cause different illnesses.

Chickenpox is easy to catch. The main symptom is spots that itch.

Rabies is a fatal virus that is common in animals such as dogs.

Colds are viruses and can bring on a sore throat, runny nose, and cough.

Protists

Protists are another kind of single-celled life form. They are very varied. Some protists are similar to fungi, animals, or plants. Some protists group together into colonies.

Food chains

Everything in the living world needs food to survive. And everything must feed on something else. This is called a food chain. Each species is part of several different food chains.

Decomposers
At the start and end of every food chain there are decomposers, such as earthworms, fungi, and dung beetles. They help break down dead animals and plants, releasing the nutrients back into the soil.

Producers
Plants such as acacia trees or grasses get their energy from the Sun and nutrients from the soil. They are known as producers.

Herbivores
Herbivores such as impala or zebra eat the plants. They do not eat meat.

What carnivorous plant can catch and eat mice and rats?

Scavengers

Dead meat, known as carrion, is eaten by scavengers such as hyenas, vultures, and bald eagles. These creatures rarely kill for food – they find animals that have already died and eat other animals' leftovers.

Carnivores

Carnivores only eat meat. On the African plains, carnivores include lions, leopards, and cheetahs.

Sea food

The further you go up the chain, the fewer animals there are. So in the sea, there are countless plankton, fewer fish, just a few seals, and even fewer polar bears.

Polar bear

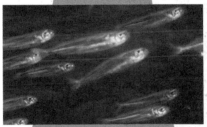

Seal

Fish

Zooplankton

Phytoplankton

Sea food

Some species of pitcher plant found in the Philippines.

Ecosystems

All over the world, living things exist in distinct kinds of places called ecosystems. Each has its own climate, soil, and complex community of plants and animals. Oceans and deserts have their own ecosystems.

Natural variety

There are different ecosystems all over the world, and the animals and plants in each one are adapted to its conditions.

Forests

Wherever there is enough rain, forests grow, and they provide homes for a huge range of plants and animals.

Oceans

More than 70 per cent of the Earth's surface is covered by ocean, which contains many different habitats.

Rivers and lakes

Freshwater ecosystems exist in pools, lakes, rivers, and streams. They are found over most of the world's land surface.

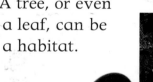

Polar and tundra

The freezing polar lands are at the far north and south of Earth, in the Arctic and Antarctic. At the edges farthest away from the poles, they merge into warmer tundra areas.

Homes sweet homes

One ecosystem contains a number of habitats. A habitat is the natural home of a particular plant or animal. A tree, or even a leaf, can be a habitat.

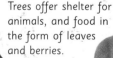

Trees offer shelter for animals, and food in the form of leaves and berries.

Are there any types of forest ecosystems other than tropical rainforests?

Mountains

Climate conditions change as you go up a mountain, so different ecosystems can exist here.

Seashores

Seashore ecosystems are half land and half sea. They change as the tide comes in and out.

Grasslands

Humans evolved in grassland habitats, and today, the largest and fastest land animals live here.

Deserts

They can be hot or cold, but deserts are always dry, with little rain. Only a few animals and plants survive here.

Living together

A group of living things in a habitat is called a community. Each one contains plants, animals, and other organisms that all rely on each other.

Ferns grow and absorb nutrients from the soil.

Snails feed on the leaves of plants, and provide food for other animals.

Frogspawn hatches into tadpoles. Some of these are eaten by other water creatures.

Rotting leaves and wood are home to fungi and small animals, such as beetles and slugs.

Frogs, which eat insects, live both on land and in the water.

Curiosity quiz

Look through the Ecosystems and habitats pages and see if you can find the pictures below.

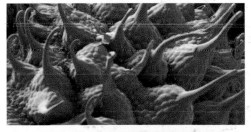

Become an expert

154-155 Food chains
222-223 All living things

Yes, deciduous woodlands and cold coniferous forests.

Polar regions

Polar regions are often dark, blasted by freezing winds, and they receive little rain. Only the toughest can survive.

Polar bears have thick blubber under their skin to help keep the cold out.

Polar bear

Although their fur is white, polar bears have black skin.

Let's stay warm
Penguins huddle together to stay warm. The adults and chicks on the outside of the huddle aren't so well protected from the cold, so they take turns standing in the middle.

Polar giants
Large animals lose heat more slowly than small ones, so many Arctic animals are big. A male polar bear can be 2.5 m (8 ft) long and weigh 800 kg (0.8 ton).

To survive blizzards, musk oxen simply sit down and wait, using as little energy as possible.

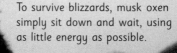

Musk oxen may look like cattle, but they are actually goats!

A walking coat
The musk ox looks like a small, shaggy-haired buffalo. Its coat, said to be eight times warmer than sheep's wool, is made of coarse hairs as long as your arm.

What is the world's largest bear?

One big cover up

Many polar animals have thick coats. The snowy owl has feathers on its body that grow long enough to cover its legs and its bill.

Snowy owl

A fine fur coat

The Arctic fox's luxurious fur even covers the soles of its feet. This fox is dark in the summer, and white in the winter. In the summer it is very busy, collecting and storing food for the winter.

Cushion growth

It's not just animals that need to wrap up warm – plants do too. Purple saxifrage has lots of tiny, overlapping leaves that completely cover the short stems.

The snowy owl's talons are perfectly shaped for gripping a lemming.

Purple saxifrage is one of the first Arctic plants to flower when the snow melts in June.

Polar regions are dark for half the year, but many animals survive.

Become an expert
8-9 The Arctic
56-57 Antarctica
170-171 Desert regions

Lemmings cope with the cold by staying in tunnels below the snow, where they hunt for plant roots to nibble. If they emerge, they may well be caught by a passing snowy owl.

The polar bear.

Deciduous forests

Deciduous trees lose their leaves in winter. These trees need weather patterns that are neither too hot nor too cold, and with seasons.

Layer on layer

Deciduous forests have two or three layers: a canopy (treetops), sometimes a layer of shrubs, and then the low-lying plants such as mosses, ferns, and spring flowers.

If conditions are right, mosses will grow on the north side of a forest tree.

Springing to life

A forest appears to sleep in winter, but in spring it bursts into life. Buds open and ferns spread out to soak up the light.

Land of plenty

A forest floor is littered with dead leaves and wood, and there are often plenty of nuts and berries — it's a perfect hunting ground for squirrels.

The grey squirrel will collect and store acorns and other seeds.

Why do squirrels have bushy tails?

Links in a chain

Food chains connect a species with what it eats.

Leaves act like solar panels to gather sunlight to make food.

Caterpillars – and many other insects – chew on leaves. That's their food.

Birds hunt caterpillars, especially in spring when they have chicks to feed.

Foxes prey on birds, small mammals, and other creatures.

Autumn colours

In the growing season, deciduous leaves appear green because of a chemical called chlorophyll. In autumn, the leaves turn yellow, brown, or red as the chlorophyll is destroyed.

Maple leaf

A leaf is a tree's food factory. In autumn, it begins to shut down.

Woodpeckers have thick skulls to protect against the shock as they hammer into wood.

Woodpecker

Making an entrance

Woodpeckers use their beaks to dig out grubs and to make nest holes. They have amazingly long tongues to probe and seek out insects.

Trees as homes

Woodpeckers take two to three weeks to dig out a nest hole, into which the female lays several eggs. The hole is usually in a dead tree.

When mature, a fern bud unrolls and the leaflets open out.

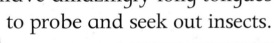

A squirrel's tail helps it to balance as it leaps from tree to tree.

Rainforests

Tropical rainforests are rich habitats for a huge variety of plants and animals. Enter a hot, damp, and shady world.

Parakeet

Time for the umbrella

A rainforest is warm and sticky, with frequent downpours. The trees take up much of the rain, but water vapour soon evaporates from their leaves, filling the air with moisture.

Queen Alexandra birdwing butterfly (female)

Orang-utan

Bursting with life

Tropical rainforests cover just 7% of Earth's land, yet contain over half of the world's species.

Beetles One scientist found 18,000 species of beetles in one small area of rainforest.

Trees A football pitch-sized patch of rainforest may contain 300 trees.

Orchids New orchids are continually being discovered in rainforests.

Birds The Amazon alone contains a third of Earth's 9,000 known bird species.

Slipper orchid

Where do most of a rainforest's animals live?

Rainforest layers

A rainforest is like a block of flats, with different residents at different layers. There are four main levels.

Emergents are the high tree tops that poke out above everything else.

The canopy is made up from the majority of the tree tops. It is a forest's leaky roof.

The understorey is made up of short trees, shade-loving plants, and lianas.

The forest floor is a thick carpet of dead leaves, ferns, and the buttresses of tree roots.

Who lives there?

All sorts of animals make the rainforest their home.

Bushbaby

Bushbabies venture out at night. Their huge eyes help them see in the dark.

Cloud forest

In mountainous areas, rainforests may be so high that they're cloaked in clouds. The heavy moisture encourages lush plant growth.

These frogs eat poisonous insects, then store the poison in their skin. Their colourful patterns let other animals know that they are dangerous to eat.

Blue poison dart frog

Yellow-banded poison dart frog

Eastern rosella

Moth orchid

Become an expert

156-157 Ecosystems
160-161 Deciduous forest

Constrictors don't have fangs or poison, so they kill prey by squeezing it to death.

Boa constrictor

Most of a rainforest's animals (excluding worms in the leaf litter) live in the canopy.

A sea of grass

Most plants grow from the top, but grass grows from the bottom. This means it can grow back if it's eaten, or if it is flattened by being trampled.

Grass is resistant to being trampled by hooves.

Grass clump

Grass shedding seed

Grass seed

Grass plants use the wind to spread their pollen (the fine dust that passes from male flowers to female flowers) and their seeds.

In summer, clouds of grass pollen give some people hay fever.

The cycle of life

Tropical grasslands have wet and dry seasons. In the dry season, the grass turns straw-coloured and dies. With the rainy season, it springs back to life.

Cheetah

How old are the baobab trees in Africa?

The grass we eat

Grass doesn't just provide food for animals, it provides food for us. In fact, most people's main food comes from grasses.

Sugar is produced from sugar cane, a giant tropical grass.

Maize is used for all sorts of food products, including tortillas.

Wheat is used for flour to make bread and cakes, and for pasta.

Rice is a major food in Asia, and is eaten around the world.

Rye is mixed with wheat to make a heavy flour that is used for bread.

Texas bluebonnet

Spring flowers

While tropical grasslands burst into life in the rainy season, northern grasslands burst to life in the spring. The fields often contain colourful flowers.

Goosegrass seed

Grass attack

Walk through grass and you may find seeds clinging to your clothes. Some seeds cling on with tiny hooks that work like Velcro.

Grassland trees often have flat bottoms, where animals have grazed.

Acacia tree

Giraffe

Baobab trees

In Africa, the baobab tree survives the blistering heat of the dry season by swelling and storing water in its trunk.

Some of them have been growing there for 3,000 years.

Weeds and wildflowers

Wildflowers are pretty, but some spread so rapidly they can be troublesome to farmers.

Ragwort is immensely poisonous to horses, ponies, donkeys, and cattle.

Thistle fruits have parachutes. The seeds may be carried far and wide.

Daisies hug the ground and do well in short grass. – such as on a lawn.

Cowslip is found in clearings and at the edge of woodland as well as in meadows.

Musk mallow produces pretty flowers from June to September.

Lady's bedstraw produces tiny, star-shaped flowers.

Field scabious can produce some 2,000 seeds per plant.

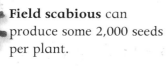

Clover is useful to farmers as it helps fertilize the soil. It is part of the pea family.

Dandelion heads are full of tiny petals, each of which turns into a seed.

Wood cranesbill is a woodland flower, but grows in hay meadows.

Buttercup flowers produce 30 seeds, so a large plant may have 22,000 seeds.

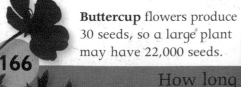

Life in a meadow

In summer, a healthy grass meadow is like a jungle in miniature. It is packed with different plants and animals.

Hidden away

A meadow may be inhabited by moles – almost blind creatures that remain below the ground.

European mole

Under the surface

Moles are capable miners, tunnelling long passages through the soil and producing tell-tale mounds of earth.

Campion flower

Watch out!

Crab spiders are powerful enough to catch bees and butterflies. They hide among the flowers, pouncing when prey comes close.

Crab spider

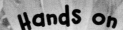

Hands on

 Make yourself a miniature meadow inside a jar. Sprinkle a few seeds onto damp soil. Put the jar on a windowsill, keep it watered, and watch as the seeds grow.

How long can a slow worm live: one, five, or 50 years?

From flower to seed

Dandelions are frequently seen in meadows, as they have a way of spreading their seeds that is incredibly successful. Each seed has a parachute, to carry it far away.

Dandelion seeds

The flower is ready to be pollinated by an insect.

The petals have died and the parachutes are forming.

A breeze lifts the parachutes. They may travel far.

Tiny monkeys

Harvest mice climb through the stems as ably as monkeys climb through trees. They build tennis ball-sized nests.

Harvest mouse

A harvest mouse weighs no more than a teaspoonful of sugar.

Bubble blower

Froghopper nymphs create damp bubbles of sticky fluid to stop themselves from drying out. The bubble also protects the nymphs from being eaten.

There are many different types of snails and a meadow is a good place to find a selection.

Slow but steady

The slow worm is not actually a worm – it's a type of lizard, but it has no legs! This one is hunting for a tasty worm or a snail.

Slow worm

It can live for more than 50 years.

At the water hole

Meet my companion
Large animals often appear at a water hole with accompanying oxpeckers. These birds help the animal keep insects at bay, picking off ticks and leeches.

During the dry season in the savanna, the only reliable place to find water is at a water hole. It can be a busy place.

Impala

As well as insect control, oxpeckers clean up any wounds the host animal may have.

Red-billed oxpecker

That's better!
When a warthog takes a bath, it ends up dirtier than ever. The mud helps it to cool down and may help get rid of fleas and other nasty insects that infect the animal's skin.

Guinea fowl

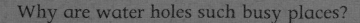

Why are water holes such busy places?

Water birds

Birds are often seen wading in waterholes, looking for fish and frogs. There are many different types, and a few are shown here.

 Yellow-billed storks stir the water with a foot to disturb fish and frogs.

 Saddle-billed storks are the largest storks, with a wingspan of 2.7 m (9 ft).

 Crowned cranes are the only cranes able to perch in trees.

 Wattled cranes surround their large nests with moat-like water channels.

Stuck in the mud
Some water holes dry up in the dry season. The African lungfish buries itself in a sticky bag of slime and hibernates until the rains come back.

A never-ending thirst

Animals visit a water hole frequently, especially elephants. Elephants have to drink about 200 litres (53 gallons) a day.

A water hole is a cool place.

African elephant

Impala

Become an expert
154-155 Food chains
164-165 A sea of grass

In the dry season, a water hole may provide the only water for miles around.

Desert regions

Deserts are Earth's driest places, with hardly any rainfall. Many of them are boiling hot – but deserts can also be very cold places, such as Antarctica.

Deserts of the world

A quarter of our world is made up of hot deserts, the biggest one being the Sahara Desert in northern Africa.

Weird weather
During the day, many deserts are scorchingly hot. At night, they can get incredibly cold. They often have huge sandstorms – or snow storms.

Animals survivors
Few plants can survive in the desert and so many animals are meat eaters. Many deserts are also so hot that a large number of animals retreat underground during the day, hunting at night.

How tall is the tallest cactus on record?

Desert records

Hot and cold deserts are full of extremes, so they hold quite a few impressive records.

Coldest desert: Antarctica is the coldest (and driest) desert.

Hottest desert: the Sahara Desert is the hottest in the world.

Biggest hot desert: the Sahara Desert covers one third of Africa.

Rainfall: a desert must have less than 2.5 cm (10 in) of rain per year.

Driest hot desert: is the Atacama Desert in South America.

Some cacti have spines instead of leaves, some have hairs. Spines protect the cactus from being eaten by animals.

Cactus

Animal survivors

Desert animals have had to develop ways to keep cool and watered.

Tiger salamander

Night hunters

During the day, salamanders hide in deep underground burrows. They come out at night and feed on worms, insects, or other salamanders.

A camel's hump contains fat that con be broken down to releases water.

Camel

Big thirst

A camel can survive for about three weeks without water. When it does drink, it can take in a huge amount.

Plant survivors

It is very difficult for plants to survive without much rainfall. The cactus is a clever plant because it collects water when it rains and stores it for dry periods.

to 20 m (63 ft) in the Sonoran Desert.

One Cardon cactus grew

Life in thin air

Walk up a mountain and you'll find that the habitat begins to change the higher you go. It also gets harder to breathe.

Become an expert
156-157 Ecosystems
160-161 Deciduous forests
166-167 Life in a meadow

Mountain zones

A temperate mountain (a mountain in a cool part of the world) has distinct zones, each with its own wildlife.

A rare sight

There are thought to be fewer than 380 wild mountain gorillas. Although they look fearsome, gorillas are peaceful vegetarians.

Mountain gorilla

Alpine zone

In cool parts of the world, mountain peaks have a permanent coating of snow. Nothing grows at this height.

Alpine meadows

In the spring, as the snow begins to melt, lush meadows come alive with flowers. This zone is above the treeline.

Conifer trees

Conifers are adapted to surviving extreme cold. Even their shape protects against the weight of the snow.

Deciduous trees

Below the conifer trees, where the air gets a little warmer, grow the deciduous trees.

Alpine marmot

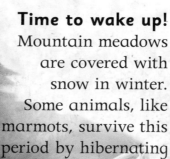

Time to wake up!

Mountain meadows are covered with snow in winter. Some animals, like marmots, survive this period by hibernating in burrows.

What is the meaning of the word "alpine"?

Rock gardens

When the snow melts in spring, the grassy meadows on high mountains are ablaze with flowers.

Mountain daisy These bloom in their thousands across alpine meadows.

Rock spiraea Creamy-white flowers form dense mats over rocky areas.

Thyme Low, thick clumps of miniature thyme make a colourful appearance.

Saxifrage There are many different colours of this hardy plant.

Edelweiss In many places, this plant is now protected: you can't pick it.

Alpine snowbell Tiny bell-shaped flowers push their way up in early spring.

Gelada baboons

Who needs a tree!

Some monkeys prefer cliffs to trees! Gelada baboons actually sleep on cliffs, perched on the narrowest ledges.

Ibex

This is my home

Ibex are goats. They can scramble up the steepest slopes and leap about without losing their footing.

Alpine chough

Life in thin air

Mountain air is so thin that mountaineers need oxygen tanks, but birds like the chough have no problem breathing it. A chough once accompanied a climbing expedition to the summit of Mount Everest.

Above the treeline and below permanent snow.

Cool caves

A large cave will take thousands of years to form. From insects to bats, many animals find a cave a good place to live.

Stalactite

A dripping start

Caves are often damp, if not wet. Stalactites form drip by drip as minerals are deposited by water dripping from the roof.

A stalactite forms from the roof down.

Long-eared bat

I hear you!

Many bats have poor sight, but incredibly good hearing. They hunt by making squeaks and clicks that bounce off prey, telling the bat the prey's location.

Webbed skin for flight.

Cave spider

Feel the way

Like bats, cave spiders cannot see well. To compensate, they have a strongly developed sense of touch to help them move around – and catch prey.

What's the name for a person that lives only in caves?

All in white

Many cave dwellers, such as cave crayfish, are white because they need no protection from the Sun's rays.

Drops of moisture show the bat is hibernating in a cold, damp cave.

Natterer's bat

Hunting for a snack

This south-east Asian snake will slip into caves because it knows there are tasty frogs, bats, and lizards to eat. Its slightly flat belly helps it to glide over rocks.

Sleep time

A cool cave is an ideal place for this bat to choose for its winter hibernation.

Red-tailed racer

A success story

Cockroaches are among the most successful of all living things, having inhabited Earth for more than 320 million years. Caves are just one of the habitats in which they thrive.

Cockroach

A troglodyte.

The flowing current

From foamy white, cascading torrents to slow but ever-moving waters, rivers provide a rich habitat for a wide variety of wildlife.

The food chain begins

As leaves and dead animals fall into the waters, bacteria multiply. This brings food for aquatic larvae such as the caddisfly.

Caddisfly larva

Caddisfly

Mosses often grow on riverside rocks and trees and provide shelter for many tiny bugs that need damp conditions.

From small beginnings

Many rivers start life as fast-flowing streams. It is often a barren beginning, but plants and animals soon thrive.

Stop that water!

Beavers sometimes build dams to create lakes, slowing the flow of water and so changing their habitat. They also create lodges to live in.

Fallen trees can provide pathways for animals and insects to cross a fast-flowing stream.

Beaver

Which is the world's longest river?

The Colorado River

Changing the landscape

Over millions of years, rivers cut channels in the earth. A notable example of this is the Colorado River and the Grand Canyon.

A brown bear is drawn to the river by the presence of salmon.

Brown bear

The fish is held in the bird's dagger-like beak.

Got it!

Many birds make a slow-moving river their hunting ground, snatching small fish from the water. The kingfisher is a colourful inhabitant of many European rivers.

Against the flow

Swift-flowing water captures oxygen, helping fish to breathe. Chinook salmon swim against the current heading for their spawning grounds. It's a dangerous journey.

The kingfisher will dive to about 25 cm (10 in) to grab a fish.

The Nile, in Africa, at 6,695 km (4,160 miles).

Still waters

A freshwater lake is a large body of standing water. Lakes support a wide variety of life, especially at their edges.

Water hyacinth

Just floating around

Plants that float do well in still water, but they can take over. Water hyacinth looks pretty, but it is a fast-growing weed and can choke other life under a thick mat.

Floating plants such as water lettuce provide shade for a lake's creatures.

Water lettuce

Cat in the water

Catfish are named for their barbels, cat-like whiskers that allow them to feel their way in murky water.

Bullhead catfish

Some species of catfish can grow to be more than 3 m (10 ft) in length.

Barbels help the fish to seek out prey. In the case of a large catfish, this may be a duck.

Medicinal leech

Horse leech

Is it a sucker?

Paddle in a muddy lake and you may emerge to find a leech on your foot. Some, but not all, leeches suck blood.

Which is the world's largest freshwater lake?

Is it a lake?

Lakes form in hollows, but not all are natural. A reservoir is a man-made lake, formed by a dam.

Ospreys are large birds of prey, reaching 1.7 m (5.5 ft) wingtip to wingtip.

A bulrush's flowers bloom on spikes and attract insects.

Attacks from above

Ospreys are found on all continents except Antarctica. They will nest near a lake or river, and swoop down to pluck fish from the water.

Pike

Life on the edge

Bulrushes and reeds often form a thick bed at a lake's edge. Known as emergents, they grow up from the lake floor and out into the air.

The ambush specialist

Pike are adept at ambushing their prey, lying in wait and nabbing passing frogs, fish, and insects.

Dragonflies are frequently seen on the plants at a lake's edge.

Don't mess with me!

The fearsome looking alligator snapping turtle is the world's largest freshwater turtle. Some have weighed in at more than 100 kg (220 lbs).

A slice of history

The common loon's ancestors lived on Earth some 65 million years ago. This red-eyed bird can dive to an incredible 27 m (90 ft) in search of food.

A pufferfish sucks in water to swell its body.

Pufferfish

The BIG escape!

If threatened, a pufferfish may blow itself up with water to stop it being swallowed by a predator, but most predators know to avoid these highly toxic fish.

Jellyfish protect themselves with stinging cells on their tentacles, but these don't stop a turtle!

Swim for my supper

Sea creatures such as the leatherback turtle will travel thousands of miles in search of jellyfish. If the food doesn't come to you, you have to go and find it!

The lion's mane jellyfish is one of the largest of all jellyfish.

Become an expert

132-133 Water mammals
144-145 The world of fish

It's a production line

Velvet crab

Many sea creatures produce hundreds or even thousands of eggs to ensure some will survive. Turtles will lay 100 eggs at once, while a velvet crab may produce 180,000 eggs!

Which of the creatures on this page has the longest history on Earth?

Survival in the sea

The ocean can be a dangerous place and sea creatures have developed a number of clever techniques to increase their chances of staying alive.

On guard!

Some sea creatures will sting or attack if threatened. Lionfish spines contain venom that can stop a fish moving or kill it. Divers are careful not to touch lionfish.

Blending in

Many of the ocean's inhabitants are masters of disguise.

Stonefish have lumpy, mottled skin that blends perfectly with the sea floor.

Pipefish swim upright, making them almost invisible amongst seagrass.

Leopard sharks have a patterning on their skin that helps them to hide.

Lost in the crowd

Many fish swim together in shoals. When they all start moving at the same speed and in the same direction to confuse predators, it is called "schooling".

Jellyfish are survivors. There were jellyfish in the oceans 650 million years ago.

What is a dinosaur?

Two legs or four? Meat-eater or planteater? What made a dinosaur? They all had four limbs, though many walked on two. There were a number of other features they had in common.

Giganotosaurus

Long tails
Scientists believe dinosaurs held their tails above the ground as there is no evidence of drag marks when trackways have been found.

Scaly skin
Impressions of dinosaur skin are rare, but palaeontologists (scientists who study fossils) have found enough to know that dinosaurs had scaly skin, rather like crocodiles today.

Meat-eating dinosaurs were known as theropods.

Cold-blooded lizards have to warm up in sunlight; they cannot control their temperature.

All dinosaurs lived on land. They could not fly or swim.

Were dinosaurs warm-blooded?
It's possible that meat-eating dinosaurs were warm-blooded (like we are), while plant-eating sauropods were cold-blooded. Warm-blooded animals use food as fuel to stay warm. Sauropods were too large to have eaten enough plants to do this.

Are dinosaurs lizards?

Giganotosaurus skulls had huge "windows".

Skull holes

Dinosaur skulls had large holes, or "windows". These made them lighter, which was necessary as some of the largest skulls were almost as long as a car.

Meat-eaters had sharp claws.

Plant-eaters had blunt toenails.

Clue in the claws

Meat-eating dinosaurs were known as theropods, which means "beast-footed", because they had sharp, hooked claws on their toes. Plant-eating dinosaurs tended to have blunt hooves or toenails.

Walking tall

Dinosaurs walked on their toes with their legs directly under their bodies.

Dinosaurs walked on upright, pillar-like legs.

Crocodiles stand with their knees and elbows slightly bent.

Lizards sprawl, with their knees and elbows held at right angles to their bodies.

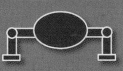

Egg layers

All dinosaurs laid eggs – some in nests, just as birds do today. The baby developed in the egg until it was ready to hatch. About 40 kinds of dinosaur eggs have been discovered.

No. They are related, but the two groups are different.

Find a friend

Many male animals today compete to win a mate. Stags crash their antlers together, while birds display colourful feathers. Scientists believe dinosaurs had to compete in similar ways.

Courtship displays tell females which males are strong and likely to make healthy young.

What did they do?

Dinosaurs may have used their head crests to show off, just like a peacock uses its colourful tail feathers.

Corythosaurus

Peacock

Pachycephalosaurus

Bone head

Pachycephalosaurus's head was 80 cm (2.5 ft) long. The dome was made of solid bone as thick as a bowling ball.

Pachycephalosaurus skull

This dinosaur had bony spikes on its head and snout.

Fighting fit

During the breeding season, male *Pachycephalosaurus* may have butted each other in fights over females. Their backbones were adapted to absorb shock.

Where did *Pachycephalosaurus* live?

Did they talk?

Nobody knows if dinosaurs made sounds, but we suspect they did. *Parasaurolophus,* a hadrosaur, may have done this by blowing air through its crest.

Crest

Become an expert
194-195
Cretaceous cows

Parasaurolophus skull

Lambeosaurus skull

Hypacrosaurus skull

Other hadrosaurs had different-shaped crests, suggesting they made different sounds.

Parasaurolophus

Brachylophosaurus

Crest

Talk like a frog

Brachylophosaurus had a short, solid crest. It may have had an inflatable pouch on the outside of this that could be used to make noises, a bit like a frog's throat pouch.

Throat pouch

In the forests of North America.

189

Eggstraordinary eggs

Scientists have been lucky enough to find lots of fossilized dinosaur eggs, and even nests. There is a huge variety of sizes and shapes, from small, circular eggs that would fit into the palm of your hand to eggs the size of cannonballs.

The largest?

This massive egg was found in China and is thought to have been laid by a *Therizinosaur*. There were larger eggs – the largest was laid by a dinosaur called *Macroelongatoolithus*.

This dinosaur egg fossil is from Mongolia.

A muddy home

Some eggs were laid in mud, which proved a perfect base for fossilization. These are *Maiasaura* eggs from Montana, USA.

Shaped like an egg?

Some dinosaur eggs were round, but others were elongated, rather like a loaf of bread.

This is a hen's egg: it shows just how large the *Therizinosaur* egg was.

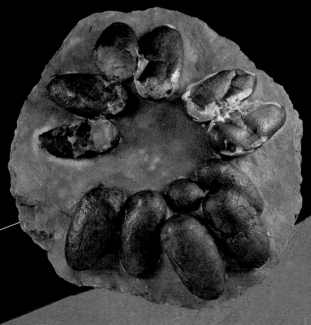

Oviraptor nest from China, showing the eggs laid in a spiral pattern. Each egg is approximately 16 cm (6 in) long.

Were dinosaur egg shells soft and leathery like those of snakes?

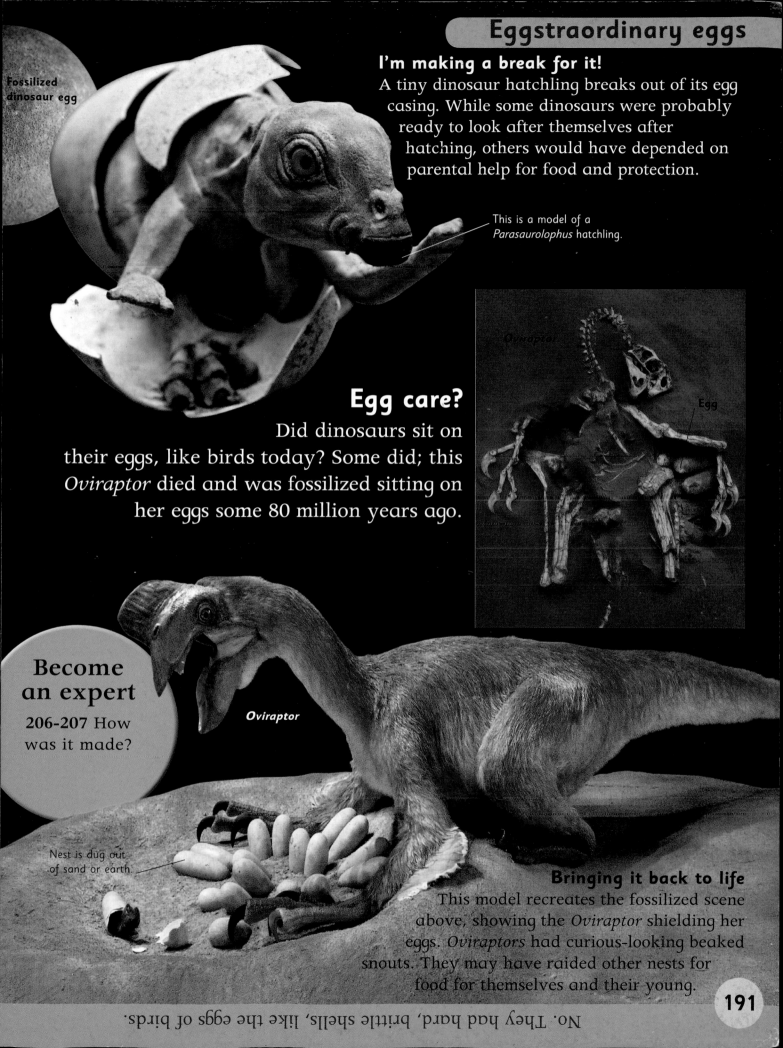

Eggstraordinary eggs

Fossilized
dinosaur egg

I'm making a break for it!
A tiny dinosaur hatchling breaks out of its egg casing. While some dinosaurs were probably ready to look after themselves after hatching, others would have depended on parental help for food and protection.

This is a model of a
Parasaurolophus hatchling.

Oviraptor

Egg

Egg care?
Did dinosaurs sit on their eggs, like birds today? Some did; this *Oviraptor* died and was fossilized sitting on her eggs some 80 million years ago.

Become an expert
206-207 How was it made?

Oviraptor

Nest is dug out of sand or earth

Bringing it back to life
This model recreates the fossilized scene above, showing the *Oviraptor* shielding her eggs. *Oviraptors* had curious-looking beaked snouts. They may have raided other nests for food for themselves and their young.

No. They had hard, brittle shells, like the eggs of birds.

Sauropods

Sauropods were the heaviest, longest, and tallest animals ever to walk on land. They were herbivores, and would have had to graze continually.

Around the world

Sauropods have been found all over the world.

Mamenchisaurus grew to 22 m (72 ft) in length in Jurassic China.

Camarasaurus reached a monstrous 23 m (75 ft) in Jurassic North America.

Barapasaurus grew to lengths of 18 m (59 ft) and roamed Jurassic India.

Vulcanodon was just 6.5 m (21 ft) when it prowled Jurassic Zimbabwe.

Tiny-brained eating machines

Sauropods had tiny heads compared to their bodies. Peg-shaped teeth were used to pull up vegetation.

Diplodocus skull

Peg-shaped teeth.

Look at the size of it!

Imagine a dinosaur that was as long as a tennis court – an adult *Diplodocus* was!

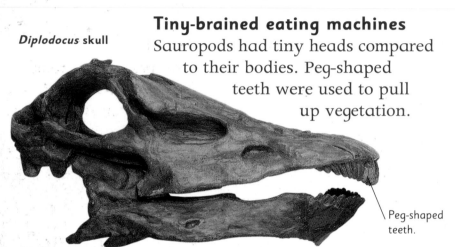

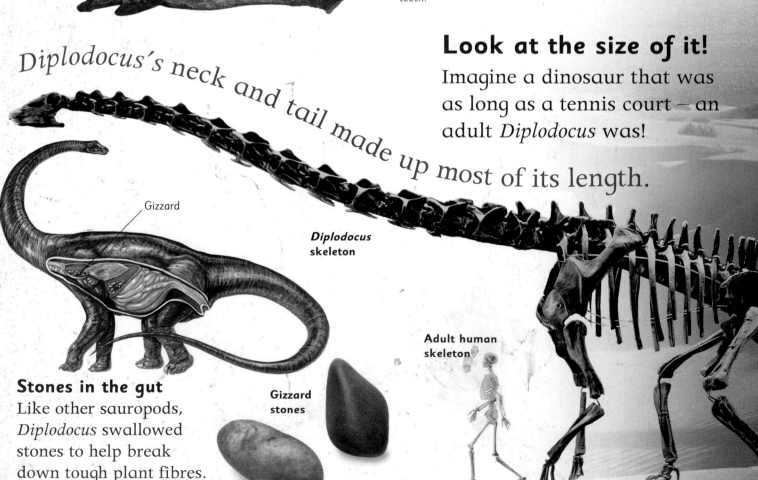

Diplodocus's neck and tail made up most of its length.

Gizzard

Diplodocus skeleton

Adult human skeleton

Stones in the gut

Like other sauropods, *Diplodocus* swallowed stones to help break down tough plant fibres.

Gizzard stones

How many neck vertebrae does the *Diplodocus* have?

It's like a giraffe!

Brachiosaurus had longer forelimbs than hind limbs so its back sloped down to its hindquarters – rather like a giraffe. But *Brachiosaurus* could reach two or three times higher than a giraffe.

Up high

Brachiosaurus nibbled leaves at the tops of trees. Its long neck may have developed so *Brachiosaurus* could feed where other plant-eaters could not reach.

Sauropods had long tails that helped to balance their bodies.

193

All sorts of crests

Those striking crests came in all sorts of different shapes.

Corythosaurus had a plate-like crest.

Tsintaosaurus' crest may have been covered in brightly coloured skin.

Lambeosaurus had a helmet-like crest.

Cretaceous cows

Hadrosaurs were basically the cows of the Cretaceous. They would have been a familiar sight in the forests and swamps of North America.

Hadrosaurs had stiff tails. It is unlikely these were swung from side to side.

Male hadrosaurs probably had larger crests than the females.

Parasaurolophus

What a sight!
Hadrosaurs are known for having some of the strangest heads of all dinosaurs many of them had a crest.

Become an expert

188-189 Find a friend
196-197 Horns and frills

Can you think of any crested animals today?

A hadrosaur had more than 1,000 teeth (though not all were in use at the same time!).

What did they eat?

One hadrosaur fossil contained the remains of its last meal: bark, pine cones, conifer needles, and branches. This tough plant matter is particularly hard to digest.

Corythosaurus

Did they have beaks?

That duck-like beak contained tightly packed rows of teeth to grind vegetation.

Fossilized hadrosaur teeth

Chew and move on

A hadrosaur such as *Corythosaurus* would have roamed in huge herds, grazing on leaves, pine needles, and ferns.

A number of lizards and birds have crests.

Horns and frills

Built like a rhinoceros, *Triceratops* is one of the best-known of all dinosaurs. It belongs to a group known as the "horned face" dinosaurs or ceratopsians.

That's one hefty plant-eater!

Three-horned face

Triceratops was one of the largest of all the horned faces, reaching about 10 m (33 ft) in length when fully grown.

196

What does the name *Triceratops* mean?

Other ceratopsians

There were a number of different dinosaurs with horns and frills.

Protoceratops, which had a head frill but lacked a horn.

Styracosaurus, or "spiked lizard", had a fancy, horned frill.

Pentaceratops had an enormous neck frill and three long horns.

Sheep of the Gobi

Protoceratops roamed the Gobi Desert in Asia rather as sheep roam today. In fact, they were about the size of sheep.

Like all the horn-face dinosaurs, *Protoceratops* had a parrot-like beak.

From baby *Protoceratops* to fully grown adult.

Fully developed skull

That's not a fighter

Protoceratops lacked any protection. Its small size would have made it the ideal prey for a number of meat-eaters.

Hatchling

One big dinosaur graveyard

The Gobi Desert is littered with the remains of *Protoceratops,* and they show all stages of growth.

T. rex

T. rex's eyeballs were the size of a clenched fist.

The mighty *T. rex* roamed North America in the last couple of million years that dinosaurs ruled the planet.

Titanic teeth

T. rex had awesome curved teeth, each as long as a human hand. Altogether it had 58 of these pointed weapons.

Hunter or scavenger?

T. rex preyed on plant-eaters such as *Triceratops*.

T. rex walked on its powerful hind limbs.

When teeth broke, new ones grew to replace them.

Was it a killer?

We don't really know if *T. rex* was a hunter or a scavenger. It may have attacked and killed, or it may have picked at dead or dying dinosaurs. It may have done both.

T. rex is short for *Tyrannosaurus rex*. What does it mean?

Lighten up

With its massive 1.5 m (5 ft) long skull, this beast could swallow small dinosaurs whole! Spaces between the skull bones made it lighter.

A *T. rex* had tiny serrations on its teeth. Its bite would have torn into a victim's flesh.

Guanlong was just 1.1 m (3.6 ft) tall, but most of that was tail and neck!

My ancestor

One of the oldest members of the tyrannosaur family was recently found in China. *Guanlong* prowled Earth some 100 million years before *T. rex*.

What a whopper!

Meet Sue, the world's largest and most complete *T. rex* skeleton. She was sold to an American museum in 1991 for a jaw-dropping GB £5.3 million (US $8 million).

Nose to tail, Sue measures 12.8 m (42 ft).

Tyrannosaurus rex means "king of the tyrant lizards".

Big and bold

Giganotosaurus means "giant southern reptile", and this dinosaur was big; in fact it may have been larger than *T. rex*. However, the two never met as *Giganotosaurus* was roaming some 10 million years before *T. rex!*

It's a new find!
Giganotosaurus bones were first unearthed in Argentina in the early 1990s, but no complete skeleton has ever been found.

Giganotosaurus would have had a keen sense of smell and excellent eyesight.

weird or what?

It's difficult to imagine just how big and heavy a fully grown *Giganotosaurus* really was. It's thought to have been as heavy as about 125 adult humans. That's a lot of people!

Where did *Giganotosaurus* live?

Let's get it!

A huge sauropod, *Argentinosaurus*, lived alongside *Giganotosaurus*. It's thought this monster may have reached 43 m (140 ft) in length. So one 13.5 m (45 ft) long *Giganotosaurus* couldn't have brought it down, but these predators may have hunted in packs.

Argentinosaurus

Become an expert

182-183 Age of the dinosaurs
192-193 Sauropods
198-199 *T. rex*

Awesome arms

Giganotosaurus had larger and more powerful forearms than *T. rex*, and they were three-fingered. They would have been used to grasp prey and food.

That's some tooth!

Giganotosaurus had large, serrated teeth for stabbing and gripping prey, and for slashing through the meat. The largest teeth were about 20 cm (8 in) in length.

In the warm swamps of Cretaceous Argentina.

Meet the raptors

Bambiraptor

Aggressive and speedy, *Velociraptor* was a formidable predator in late Cretaceous Asia. Although small, it was armed with razor-sharp teeth and terrifying dagger-like claws.

Velociraptor

The narrow jaws contained about 80 sharp teeth.

The feathers would have been used for warmth, not flight.

A feathered dinosaur?

Some dinosaur fossils have been found with traces of a feather-like covering, and it's thought that *Velociraptor* may have had feathers, though no *Velociraptor* fossil has been found with them.

The killer claw

Deinonychus also had a vicious killer claw on each of its hind legs. It held this off the ground but could slash it at victims.

Deinonychus

Experts believe that *Deinonychus* was one of the more intelligent dinosaurs.

Scientists now suspect *Deinonychus* was feathered, but the theory is so new that most models are naked.

Deinonychus
foot fossil

What does the name *Velociraptor* mean?

Deinonychus

This skeleton has been mounted to show *Deinonychus* leaping towards a victim, claws ready.

Jump and grab

Velociraptor and its relations, such as the larger *Deinonychus*, probably hunted in packs and jumped onto the back of their prey, all four limbs extended.

Deinonychus means "terrible claw".

Did you know?
Velociraptor and *Deinonychus* belong to a group called the dromaeosaurids. Scientists believe these killing machines were related to the birds alive today.

Deinonychus had a lightweight body and long hind legs.

"Speedy thief." Scientists believe it may have reached 65 km/h (40 mph).

What happened?

Sixty-five million years ago the dinosaurs died out, along with the pterosaurs and the plesiosaurs. It was a mass extinction, but what was the cause? Many believe it was the result of a meteorite.

What changed?

Scientists now believe a massive meteorite hit Earth, creating a dust cloud of noxious fumes that screened out the Sun and changed the climate.

Who died?

The extinction saw the loss of huge numbers of animals, including:

Pterosaurs, which had once filled the skies with their airborne acrobatics.

Dinosaurs, which had evolved into a huge variety of types.

Huge reptiles, which disappeared from the oceans.

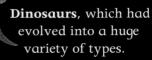

The rock would have hit Earth's crust with terrific force, sending shock waves around the world.

It was a big one!

In the early 1990s, geologists found the remains of a massive crater in Mexico. It was 180 km (112 miles) wide. They believe it was caused by a meteorite smashing into Earth 65 million years ago.

How big were the animals that survived the extinction?

Was that all?

The meteorite hit at a time of immense volcanic activity in what is now western India. This activity would have sent up clouds of ash and dust that would have blocked the Sun's light – just like the effect of the meteorite. That's two major events around the same time.

The rock that created the Mexican crater was 10 km (6 miles) in diameter.

From meteorite to volcano, the extinction may well have been a combination of conditions.

An exploding volcano sends up clouds of lethal dust.

No land animal heavier than a large dog survived.

Living dinosaurs

You may think that reptiles are closely related to dinosaurs, but dinosaurs may have more in common with birds!

A hidden link?

The link between dinosaurs and birds is a puzzle. *Caudipteryx* appears to have been a combination of bird and dinosaur.

Caudipteryx would not have been able to fly as its wings were too small.

The first bird?

The earliest-known bird is *Archaeopteryx*, which first appeared in the Jurassic period. It had the toothed head, clawed fingers, and long bony tail of a dinosaur, but it also had feathers.

Fossilized *Archaeopteryx*

Archaeopteryx means "ancient wing".

What size do you think *Archaeopteryx* reached?

Why feathers?

Feathers protect birds from water and from temperature changes, and they may have evolved on some dinosaurs for the same purpose.

Caudipteryx was a Cretaceous creature.

Feathers provide good insulation from cold.

Caudipteryx had clawed hands. It also had teeth.

Caudipteryx was about the size of a turkey.

Hoatzin are found in parts of South America.

We have claws

Some modern birds have clawed wings. Hoatzin chicks have two tiny claws at the end of each wing. These are not used in the adult, but the chicks use them to clamber through trees.

Did you know?

Although some dinosaurs had feathers, experts are still discussing the possible link between dinosaurs and birds. It does seem unlikely, though, that any dinosaur flew.

Pieces of a puzzle

More and more "dino-birds" are being discovered, and each discovery helps our understanding. This model is based on feathered fossils found in China.

It was small: about the size of a pigeon.

211

What is science?

Science is the search for truth and knowledge. It holds the key to understanding life, the Universe... and almost everything! Scientists divide science into different areas.

From atoms to space

Scientists study a huge variety of things, from the tiniest atoms that make up everything around us to the mysteries of space.

Everything you see is made up of microscopic atoms.

Life science

How do living things survive and grow, where do they live, what do they eat, and how do their bodies work? Life science seeks to answer such questions about the living world, from microscopic bacteria to plants and animals – including you!

The scientific study of plants is called botany.

Physical science

This science looks at energy and forces. There are different types of energy, including light, heat, and sound. Forces are the things that hold everything in place in our world. Without the force of gravity, for example, you would fly off into space!

We have learned how to send energy to where it is needed.

Life science studies the living world around us.

Planet Earth

What is the study of animals called?

Curiosity quiz
Look through the Planet
Earth pages and see if
you can identify each of
the picture clues below.

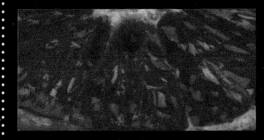

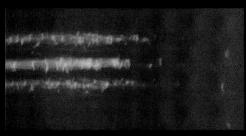

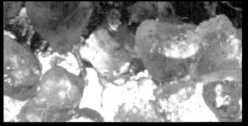

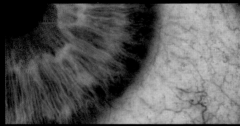

Earth and space science

Earth is a dot in a vast Universe
filled with planets and moons, stars
and galaxies. As far as we know,
Earth is special because it is the
only place that supports life. Earth
and space science is the study of
the structure of our planet   and
everything that exists beyond it.

The scientific study
of volcanoes is
called volcanology.

Materials science

Our Universe is filled with atoms
and elements, molecules, mixtures,
and compounds. Materials science
is the study of these things, how
they behave, how we use
them, and how they
react with one
another.

One branch of science studies
how materials can change.

Become
an expert

6-7 Our world
272-273 Our place
in space

Pictures of Earth from
space help scientists
understand Earth better.

Advances in science

Science begins with problems. The world's great scientists were all thinkers who wanted to solve life's problems. This need for understanding has produced many great inventions and discoveries.

Stories suggest Newton discovered gravity with an apple.

Johannes Gutenberg (1400–1468)

Gutenberg played a key role in printing. Experts believe he invented metal-type printing in Europe. Gutenberg's press was quick, accurate, and hard-wearing, compared to earlier woodblock printing.

Newton found that white light was made up of seven colours.

Gutenberg's first printed book was the Bible in 1455.

Isaac Newton (1642–1727)

Newton investigated forces and light. He realized there must be a force that keeps the planets in orbit around the Sun. Today we know this as gravity. Newton also discovered that white light is made up of all the colours of the rainbow.

1400   **1500**   **1600**

Wooden replica of da Vinci's Ornithopter.

Leonardo da Vinci (1452–1519)

Leonardo was a painter and inventor. He drew plans for helicopters, aeroplanes, and parachutes. Unfortunately, the technology of the time was not good enough to build any that worked.

Galileo Galilei (1564–1642)

Galileo proved that the Earth moves around the Sun by looking at the Solar System through a telescope. A few wise thinkers had always suspected the truth, but most people at the time believed that our Earth was the centre of everything.

Replica of a 17th-century telescope

Who invented the bifocal lens?

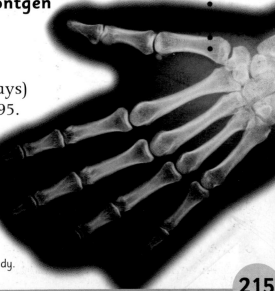

A kite helped Benjamin Franklin learn about lightning and electricity.

Did you know?

More than 2,000 years ago, Greek thinker Aristotle recommended that people look at nature, and carry out experiments to test ideas.

Inventions

Inventions and discoveries have changed the course of our history.

Wheel (3,500 BCE) The first known wheel was used in Mesopotamia.

Paper (50 BCE) This was invented in China, but kept secret for many years.

Compass (1190) The magnetic compass was first used by the Chinese.

Parachute (1783) The first one flew centuries after Leonardo made his drawings.

Steam train (1829) The earliest successful model reached 48 kph (30 mph).

Colour photo (1861) First produced by physicist James Clerk Maxwell.

Benjamin Franklin (1706–1790)

American scientist Benjamin Franklin experimented with lightning and electricity. His work in the 1700s laid the foundations for today's electrical world.

Franklin risked his life flying a kite in a storm.

Louis Pasteur (1822–1895)

Best known for discovering pasteurization (a process that uses heat to destroy bacteria in food, particularly milk), Pasteur also discovered that some diseases were caused by germs. He encouraged hospitals to be very clean to stop germs spreading.

1700

1800

William Herschel (1738–1822)

Herschel is well known for his work in astronomy (he first identified the planet Uranus). He also discovered infrared radiation – this technology is used today for wireless communications, night vision, weather forecasting, and astronomy.

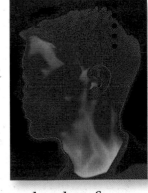

Wilhelm Conrad Röntgen (1845–1923)

Röntgen discovered electromagnetic rays (known today as x-rays) on November 8th, 1895. His important discovery earned him the first Nobel Prize in Physics in 1901.

X-rays allow doctors to look inside the human body.

Movie projectors developed quickly after Edison's early work.

Early movie projector

Karl Landsteiner (1868–1943)

Austrian-born physiologist Landsteiner discovered that human blood can be divided into four main groups – A, B, AB, and O. This laid the foundation of modern blood groupings.

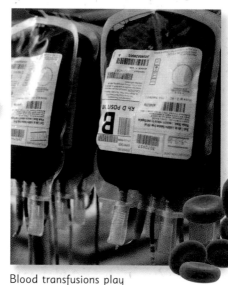

Orange juice is a good source of vitamin C.

Albert Szent-Györgyi (1893–1986)

The Hungarian scientist Albert Szent-Györgyi is best known for detecting vitamin C. He also pioneered research into how muscles move and work. He won the Noble Prize for physiology and medicine in 1937.

You inherit your blood type from your parents.

Red blood cells

Thomas Edison (1847–1931)

Thomas Alva Edison produced more than 1,000 inventions, including long-lasting light bulbs, batteries, and movie projectors.

Blood transfusions play an important part in modern medicine.

1800

1850

Albert Einstein (1879–1955)

German-born physicist Albert Einstein's famous equation $E=mc^2$ explained how energy, mass, and time are all related. It helped scientists understand how the Universe works.

$$E=mc^2$$

Einstein's equation

Earthquakes destroy homes and office buildings.

Charles Richter (1900–1985)

Richter developed a way to measure the power of earthquakes. He worked on his scale with fellow physicist Beno Gutenberg.

A "great" earthquake (8–9.9 on the Richter scale) strikes on average once a year.

Epicentre

Who invented frozen food?

Alan Turing (1912–1954)

During the Second World War, Alan Turing, a brilliant mathematician, helped develop code-breaking machines that eventually led to the invention of modern computers.

Today's computers are lightweight and portable – early models filled whole rooms.

The English used the Enigma machine to break German codes during World War II (sometimes known as WWII).

Computers (1941)

The first computers were huge machines. They couldn't cope with complicated tasks, but worked on only one thing at a time.

Mobile phones (1980s)

Developed from the two-way radios of the 40s and 50s, the first mobiles were large and heavy, weighing about 35 kg (77 lbs) – the same as a 10-year-old child.

Mobile phone

Modern inventions

Imagine the world without these fantastic inventions:

 Antibiotics The first antibiotic, penicillin, was discovered accidentally.

 Cars Some of the early models were driven by coal or wood-fired engines.

 Nuclear power is efficient, but some people think it could harm us.

 Plastics technology is used to make many of the things in your home.

 Compact disks are small and light, and they store lots of information.

 Energy-efficient light bulbs help save energy in your home.

900

DNA discovered (1953)

The identification of DNA (which holds information in human cells) led to DNA profiling, a huge help to the police – criminals can now be identified by a single hair or spot of blood.

Nuclear bombs (1945)

Sometimes science creates monsters, like the bombs the USA dropped on Japan in WWII. They killed nearly 300,000 people and ended the war.

The internet (1990s)

With its roots in the 1960s, the Internet (short for International Network) became public during the mid 90s, and is now used for fun and education by about 1.5 billion people.

Before DNA profiling, police identified criminals by their fingerprints. This system was developed in the 1890s.

Clarence Birdseye, in 1924.

Being a scientist

Scientists study the world around us. They look for gaps in our knowledge and try to find the answers. Not all scientists study the same things – they specialize in different areas.

Experiments can involve toxic fumes or chemicals that might explode, so scientists wear protective goggles.

Testing, testing

Scientists explore their ideas and theories using tests called experiments. In this book, there are lots of "hands-on" experiments you can do to try things out for yourself.

Mixing it up

Experimenting with chemicals and their reactions can produce some mixed results. Some mixtures can be dangerous, while others can be the answer the scientists are after.

How much bigger do things look through a microscope?

A closer look

Hooke's microscope

During the 17th century, the microscope was developed by Dutchman Anton van Leeuwenhoek and refined by Robert Hooke in England. Early models revealed the tiny organisms in water, while modern versions can look inside a single cell.

Inside view

When you go to hospital, the doctor may send you for a body scan. Using a powerful machine, the medical team can see what's going on inside you.

Hands on

Fill a cup or vase with water, and add a few drops of food colouring. Cut the end off the stem of a flower and put the flower in the water.

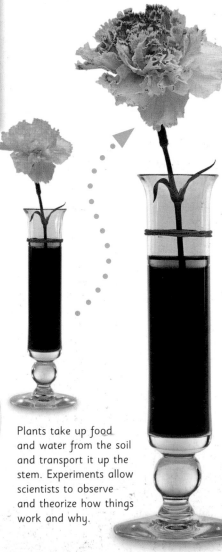

Plants take up food and water from the soil and transport it up the stem. Experiments allow scientists to observe and theorize how things work and why.

Types of scientist

Almost everything in the world is the subject of study by a scientific specialist.

Zoologists study animals of all kinds, except for human beings.

Biologists are interested in everything about life and living organisms.

Paleontologists know about fossils, and try to learn from them.

Botanists learn about the world of plants, plant types, and plant groups.

Chemists study elements and chemicals, and they help make new substances.

Astronomers are experts on space, the planets, the stars, and the Universe.

Entomologists are a special kind of zoologist who learn about insects.

Geologists find out about our Earth, particularly by studying rocks.

Archaeologists are interested in the remains of past peoples and lives.

Ecologists study the relationship between living things and their environment.

Oceanographers know all about ocean life and landscapes.

Science and everyday life

Science is not just used by experts working in laboratories. It is part of all our lives. From brushing your teeth to setting your alarm, science is with you all day, every day.

Teflon

Invented in 1938, Teflon was used in space suits. In everyday life it stops stuff sticking to hot surfaces.

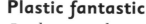

Iron

Teflon pan

Electricity

Electricity lights up the world and gives us the energy to cook, travel, work, and play.

Cities at night are bright places, lit up by office, house, and street lights.

Plastic building blocks

Plastic fantastic

Look around you and you will see dozens of things made of plastic. From containers to toys, plastic is a versatile and hard-wearing material. Some plastics can now be recycled.

Plastic medicine bottles

What was the first satellite in space?

Surgeons get a helping hand from computers.

Masks, aprons, and gloves help doctors keep operation rooms free from infection.

Satellite orbiting the earth

In the best of health

Long ago, people relied on herbs to produce cures for disease. Thanks to modern science, many illnesses that were once untreatable can now be cured or prevented.

Clothing technology

Advances in sports clothing technology have impacted on everyday clothes. Breathable fabric, stretchy spandex, and thermal underwear were developed from specialized sports and leisure clothes.

Communications

Satellites orbit the Earth, beaming back all sorts of information. They send TV signals, supply weather information, and help us gaze into space.

From here to there

Science and technology make it much easier to get around. Trains, planes, and cars make the world a smaller place and allow us to visit exotic destinations. They are also useful for getting to school on time.

As fast as a speeding bullet train...?

Bullet trains in Japan travel up to 300 kph (186 mph).

Become an expert

221

Sputnik 1. It was launched by the Soviet Union in 1957.

All living things

Carbon cycle

Green plants take in the gas carbon dioxide from the air and use it to make food, converting it into things such as carbohydrates. Animals take in some of the carbon when they eat plants.

Every living thing contains carbon. Human beings take in carbon through carbohydrates, fats, and proteins in food, and release it as carbon dioxide gas when breathing out. It is also released from dead matter, sometimes quite soon, sometimes millions of years later in fuels like oil and coal.

Carbon dioxide in the atmosphere

CARBON DIOXIDE

OXYGEN

Animals

Animals such as these sheep contribute to the carbon cycle by eating, breathing, and dropping waste. They take in carbon in the plants they eat, and release it when they breathe out. Their bodies will release more carbon when they die.

Animals breathe out carbon dioxide.

Animals eat plants and take in some carbon.

CARBON

CARBON DIOXIDE RELEASED

An animal's droppings also contribute to the carbon cycle.

In particular circumstances, carbon forms a hard crystal. What is its name?

Plants and animals die and their bodies decay.

DECOMPOSING

DECOMPOSING

DECOMPOSING

Fossil fuels
Sometimes the remains of organisms are exposed to extreme pressure and heat. Over millions of years, they turn into carbon-rich fuels, like coal and oil.

Waste disposal
When animals die, their bodies break down and decompose.

Waste fertiliser
Part of you might once have been part of a dinosaur. Why? Because like all living things, dinosaurs produced waste and their waste became a part of the never-ending carbon cycle.

Digesters
Decomposition in the soil is helped along by the endless action of worms and bacteria. These animals are an important part of the carbon cycle.

A diamond.

223

Properties of matter

What they are...

There are many different properties of matter.

Boiling point is the hottest a liquid can get before becoming a gas.

Freezing point is the temperature at which a liquid becomes a solid.

Plasticity is how well a solid can be reshaped.

Conductivity is how well a material lets electricity or heat travel through it.

Malleability is how well a solid can be shaped without breaking.

Tensile strength is how much a material can stretch without breaking.

Flammability is how easily and quickly a substance will catch fire.

Reflectivity is how well a material reflects light. Water reflects well.

Transparency is how well a material will let light pass through it.

Flexibility is how easily a material can be bent.

Solubility is how well a substance will dissolve, such as salt in water.

Some materials are hard and brittle, while others are flexible. Some materials are colourful, while others are transparent. These kinds of features are called "properties".

A cork floats on oil. Oil floats on water.

Does it float?

It's easy to learn about some properties, such as the ability to float. The amount of matter in a certain volume of an object is called its density. Objects and liquids float on liquids of a higher density and sink through liquids of a lower density.

A plastic building brick sinks through oil but floats on water.

An onion sinks through oil and water, but floats on syrup. Syrup sinks below water.

A good insulator

Heat cannot easily pass through some materials. These are known as insulators. For example, aerogel can completely block the heat of a flame. But don't try this at home!

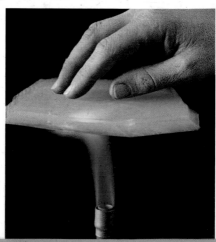

Is a diamond harder than quartz?

Safety glass

Brittleness
Some materials, such as glass, are very brittle and will break when pushed out of shape. Safety glass is designed to crack rather than break.

Hardness
A scientist called Friedrich Mohs created a scale of ten minerals to compare how hard they are. Many materials are graded on this scale.

Compressibility
Gases can be squashed, or compressed, by squeezing more into the same space. This is what happens when you pump up a tyre.

Gas can be compressed because its particles are far apart. A bicycle pump pushes the particles closer together.

Foot pump

Gas particles

Diamond is the hardest mineral.

9 Corundum

10 Diamond

5 Apatite

6 Feldspar

7 Quartz

8 Topaz

4 Fluorite

3 Calcite

2 Gypsum

1 Talc

Softest mineral

Hands on
Collect some different pebbles and put them in order of hardness. A pebble is harder than another if it scratches it. This is how Mohs worked out his scale.

A smooth flow
Some liquids flow more easily than others. It depends on their "stickiness", or viscosity. Hot lava from a volcano flows slowly because it is sticky.

Yes, a diamond is the hardest mineral of all. It will scratch quartz.

Changing states

When solids get hot enough, they melt and become liquids. When liquids get cold enough, they freeze and become solid. This is called changing states and it happens to all kinds of substances.

Liquid metal

Every substance melts and boils at a particular temperature (its melting and boiling points). Most metals are solid at everyday temperatures because they have a high melting point. But mercury has such a low melting point that it is liquid even at room temperature.

Condensation

As water vapour in the air is cooled, it changes into liquid water. This is called condensation. You can see it on the outside of a cold bottle.

Changing states of water

Water exists as a solid, liquid, or gas. You can find all three forms of water in your home. They are ice, water, and steam (water vapour).

When water vapour in the air touches a cold bottle, it condenses into tiny drops of liquid.

Ice is solid water. It forms when liquid is cooled until it freezes. Each piece of ice has a definite shape.

When ice is warmed, it melts and becomes liquid and takes on the shape of the container holding it.

As water is heated, bubbles of steam form. They rise to the surface and burst, so steam escapes into the air.

Rivers of iron

Iron must be heated in a furnace to make it melt. Molten iron is so hot it glows white. It is poured into a mould and left to harden to make solid iron objects.

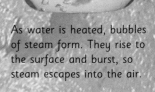

Why does chocolate become soft and gooey in your mouth?

Washing dries faster on a hot day, when heat turns water into vapour very quickly.

Evaporating
In the open air, water slowly turns into vapour – this is called evaporation. Wet clothes dry on a line because the water they hold evaporates.

Melting chocolate

Mmmm... frozen fruit inside

Freezing
Icicles are spikes of ice that form when dripping water freezes. You often see them on trees in winter. If water keeps dripping down and freezing, the icicle will get longer and longer.

Melting
When you don't eat your ice cream quickly enough, it melts and changes from a solid to a liquid! Chocolate melts too, and makes your hands all sticky. Most solids will melt if the temperature is high enough.

Become an expert...
230-231 Molecules
232-233 Reactions and changes

Because the warmth of your mouth makes it melt.

Amazing atoms

If you could keep smashing an object into smaller and smaller bits, you would eventually break it down into bits that can't get any smaller – atoms. Atoms are tiny particles that make up everything around us.

Electrons whizz around the nucleus of the atom

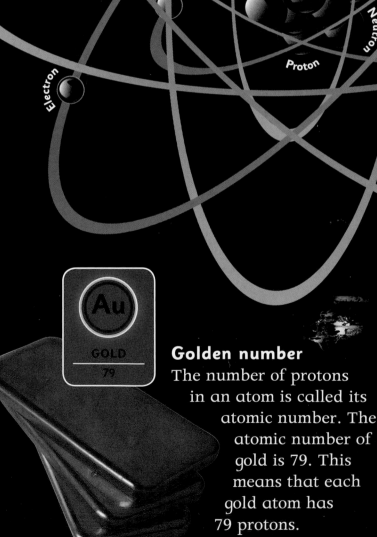

Neutron

Proton

Electron

Inside an atom

Inside an atom are three tiny types of particle: protons, neutrons, and electrons. Protons and neutrons make up the atom's nucleus (core). The electrons are outside this.

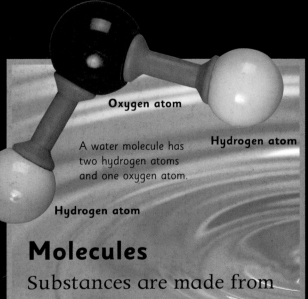

Oxygen atom

Hydrogen atom

A water molecule has two hydrogen atoms and one oxygen atom.

Hydrogen atom

Molecules

Substances are made from little groups of atoms called molecules. The molecules in water have three atoms.

Au

GOLD

79

Golden number

The number of protons in an atom is called its atomic number. The atomic number of gold is 79. This means that each gold atom has 79 protons.

How many atoms are there in a drop of water?

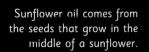

Sunflower oil comes from the seeds that grow in the middle of a sunflower.

Big molecules

In natural substances like vegetable oil, the atoms are often joined in chains to make very large molecules. The molecules in sunflower oil contain 50 atoms each.

Oxygen atom

Hydrogen atom

Carbon atom

weird or what?

An atom is mostly empty space. If an atom were the size of a sports stadium, the nucleus would be the size of a marble in the middle.

The explosion of a nuclear bomb can create a spectacular "mushroom cloud".

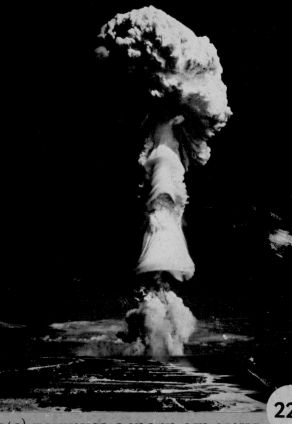

The mighty atom

When the nucleus of an atom is split, it releases a huge amount of energy. Nuclear bombs use this "atomic energy" to create huge explosions. Nuclear power stations use the energy to produce electricity.

There are about 5 sextillion (5,000,000,000,000,000,000,000,000) atoms in a grain of sand.

Molecules

In most materials, atoms are joined in tiny groups called molecules. The shapes of molecules and the way they pack together can help explain how different materials behave.

Frozen solid

Cold molecules move slowly, allowing them to pack together more easily. When water freezes, the molecules line up in neat rows, forming ice crystals.

Steaming ahead

Molecules are always jiggling about. When they get hot, they move further and faster. When water heats up, the molecules may start moving so fast that they escape into the air as water vapour.

Snow may look like white powder, but if you look closely you can see thousands of tiny crystals as clear as glass.

Clouds appear when water vapour cools down and becomes liquid again. The grey mist is made of millions of tiny liquid droplets.

Melt: As a solid heats up, its molecules move faster until they break free from each other and move separately, turning the solid into a liquid.

Solidify: As a liquid cools, its molecules lose energy and move more slowly. Eventually they start sticking together, turning the liquid into a solid.

Liquid

If a liquid is poured into a jar or bottle, it takes the shape of its container and stays in place.

Are diamonds impossible to destroy?

Diamond is made into jewels that are almost indestructible.

Diamond molecule

Diamond is the hardest natural substance known. Its hardness comes from the way the carbon atoms in each diamond are arranged. Each atom is joined by strong bonds to four neighbouring atoms.

Each group of five atoms in a diamond forms a pyramid shape. This shape makes diamond amazingly strong.

Become an expert

224-225 Properties of matter
226-227 Changing states

Graphite molecule

Graphite, like diamond, is also made of carbon atoms, but the atoms are arranged in a different way, making graphite very soft.

Each carbon atom in graphite is joined to only three neighbours. The atoms form layers that slip over each other, making graphite soft.

Graphite is used to make the soft lead in pencils.

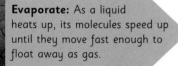

Evaporate: As a liquid heats up, its molecules speed up until they move fast enough to float away as gas.

Gas

Condense: When gas molecules lose energy and slow down, they stick together and form liquid.

A gas can fill any container it's put in. If there's no lid to seal the container, the gas will escape into the air.

No, you can burn them.

Reactions and changes

When the atoms in molecules rearrange to form new kinds of molecules, we say a chemical reaction has taken place. Chemical reactions often lead to a dramatic change.

Melting is not a chemical reaction.

Chemical change

Fire is caused by a chemical reaction. When wood burns, the atoms in wood are rearranged to form new kinds of molecules. This process releases energy as light and heat, producing glowing flames.

Physical change

Not all dramatic changes are caused by chemical reactions. When ice lollies melt, the atoms in the water molecules do not get rearranged into new molecules – they remain water molecules. Melting is simply a physical change.

Burning is a chemical reaction.

Escaping energy
Chemical reactions can release energy as heat and light. A sparkler contains chemicals that release a lot of energy as light to create a dazzling shower of sparks.

What chemical reaction makes silver objects slowly turn grey and dull?

Speeding up reactions

Cooking makes carrots softer because the heat causes a chemical reaction. Chopping carrots into small bits speeds up the reaction because it increases the area of contact between the carrots and the hot water.

Sliced carrots cook faster than whole carrots.

Glow in the dark

Light sticks glow in the dark thanks to a chemical reaction that releases energy as light. You can slow down this reaction by putting a light stick in a fridge, which makes it last longer.

Hands on

Ask an adult to boil some red cabbage and save the coloured water. Let the water cool. Then add acid (vinegar) or alkali (bicarbonate of soda) and watch for a spectacular change of colour!

Soda volcano

If you drop mints into a bottle of fizzy drink, the drink turns to foam and explodes out in an instant. This is a physical change rather than a chemical reaction. The rough surface of the mints helps gas, dissolved in the drink, to turn into bubbles much more quickly than it normally would.

Tarnishing. It happens when silver atoms react with oxygen atoms in air.

What is energy?

Energy is what makes everything happen. Your body needs energy so that you can move, grow, and keep warm. We also need energy to power our cars, light our homes, and do thousands of other jobs.

Sources of energy

Energy comes from lots of different sources.

 Wind drives wind turbines, which convert movement energy into electricity.

 Geothermal energy is heat from deep underground.

 Plants can be burnt to provide energy for cooking, heating, and lighting.

 Waves can be used to make small amounts of electricity.

 Dams harness the energy in rivers flowing downhill to make electricity.

 The Sun's energy can be captured by solar panels to make electricity.

 Fossil fuels such as oil are used to power cars and to make electricity.

Sunshine

We get nearly all our energy from the Sun. Plants absorb the energy in sunlight and store it as chemical energy. The stored energy enters our bodies as food and is released inside our body's cells. All animals and plants obtain their energy from the Sun this way.

Only a tiny fraction of the Sun's energy reaches Earth.

A bow stores energy by bending. When you let go, the bow springs back into shape and releases the stored energy.

Stored energy

An object can store energy and release it later. When you wind up a clockwork toy, energy is stored in a spring. A bow and arrow uses stored energy to shoot the arrow. Stored energy is also called potential energy because it has the potential to make things happen.

Is energy destroyed when we use it?

Movement energy

Rollercoasters start from the top of a hill, where their height gives them a lot of potential energy. As they move downhill, the potential energy turns into movement energy (kinetic energy), making them go faster and faster.

Nuclear energy

Matter is made up of tiny particles called atoms. The centre of an atom, called a nucleus, stores huge amounts of energy. This nuclear energy is used in power stations to make electricity.

Electrical energy

Lightning is caused by electrical energy in a storm cloud. The electrical energy turns into the heat and light energy of lightning and the sound energy of thunder.

Chain reactions

Changing energy from one type to another is called "energy conversion". The steps can be linked to make an energy chain.

Coal contains chemical energy.

Burning coal produces heat energy, which is used to boil water. Boiling water creates steam.

Moving steam is a form of kinetic (motion) energy, which operates turbines.

The kinetic energy produced by the moving turbines creates electricity.

Electrical energy used by television sets changes into light, sound, and heat energy.

Energy cannot be destroyed. It turns into another form of energy when it's used.

Electricity

Have you ever thought about what powers your television, your computer, or the lights in your bedroom? A flow of electricity makes all these things work.

Power supply

Electricity travels to your home along wires above and sometimes below the ground. The wires above the ground hang on metal towers called pylons.

Making electricity

Electricity is a form of energy. It can be made using any source of energy, such as coal, gas, oil, wind, or sunlight. On a wind farm, wind turbines use the energy of moving air to create electricity.

Everyday electricity

We use electricity in all sorts of ways in our everyday lives.

Heating: electricity heats up household appliances such as irons and cookers.

Lighting: electricity lights up our homes, schools, offices, and streets.

Communication: electricity can power telephones and computers.

Transport: electricity is used to power certain vehicles, such as trams.

What's the name of a small object that can store electricity?

Circuits of power

An electric circuit is a loop that electricity can travel around. An electric current moves through the wires in this circuit, and lights up the bulb.

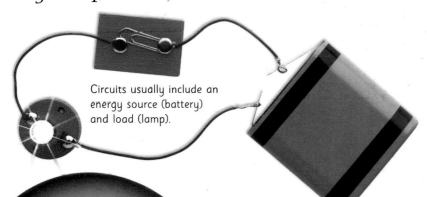

Circuits usually include an energy source (battery) and load (lamp).

Electrical cables

Electrical cables are made of metal and plastic. Electricity flows through the metal (which is called a conductor). The plastic (which is called an insulator) stops electricity escaping.

Hands on

Rub a party balloon up and down on your clothes. The balloon will now stick to the wall. This is because rubbing it gives the balloon an electric charge.

Lightning strikes

When electricity builds up in one place it is called static electricity. A bolt of lightning is a huge spark of static electricity in the sky.

High voltage

Electricity can be very dangerous. This triangle is an international warning symbol. It means "Caution: risk of electric shock".

Food battery

Food that contains water and weak acid will conduct electricity. In a food battery, a chemical reaction between the metal and the acid in the food creates an electric current.

Light

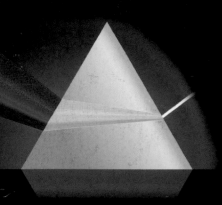

Light is a form of energy that our eyes can detect. It comes in all the colours of the rainbow, but when the colours are mixed together, light is white.

Where does light come from?

Light comes from inside atoms. When an atom needs to lose energy, it spits out the energy as a particle of light.

The light of a flame is caused by a chemical reaction that releases energy stored in the burning wax.

Casting shadows

Light can only travel in straight lines. If something blocks its path, it casts a shadow – a dark area that the light cannot reach.

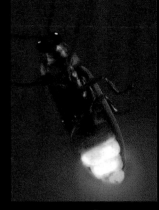

Fireflies

Some animals create their own light. Fireflies have tails that flash a yellowish-green colour at night to attract mates.

Using light

We can use light for many different things.

 CDs and DVDs store digital information that can be read by laser beam.

 Cameras capture light in a split second to create photographs.

 Telescopes magnify the light from distant stars and planets so we can see them.

 Mirrors reflect light so we can see images of ourselves.

 Periscopes bend light so we can see around corners.

 Torches shine a beam of light to help us see in the dark.

What's the fastest thing in the Universe?

Bright

Dark

Light enters your eyes through your pupils (the black circles in the middle). Pupils can change size. When it's dark they get bigger to let more light in, and when it's bright they shrink so you don't get dazzled.

How your eye works

The human eye works like a camera. The front parts of the eye focus light rays just as a camera lens does. The focused rays form an upside-down image in the back of your eyeball.

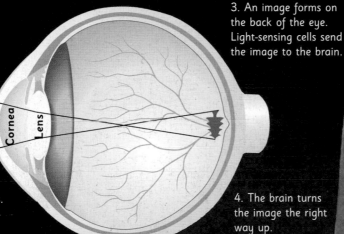

Tree

1. Light rays from the tree enter your eye.

Cornea

Lens

2. The cornea (front of eye) and lens focus the rays.

3. An image forms on the back of the eye. Light-sensing cells send the image to the brain.

4. The brain turns the image the right way up.

Reflecting light

When light hits a mirror, it bounces straight back off. If you look into a mirror, you see this bounced light as a reflection.

Convex mirrors bulge outwards. They make things look smaller but let you see a wider area.

Concave mirrors bulge inwards. They make things look bigger but show a smaller area.

Light beams

Unless it enters your eyes, light is invisible. The beam of light from a lighthouse can only be seen from the side if it catches mist or dust in the air, causing some of the light rays to bounce off towards you. Lighthouse beams sweep round in circles and can be seen from far out at sea.

Light. It travels at a thousand millions kph (620,000,000 mph).

Sound

Every sound starts with a vibration, like the quivering of a guitar string. The vibration squeezes and stretches the air between the vibrating object and your ear. This is a sound wave.

Hands on

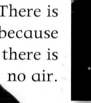

When you blow across a bottle, the air inside vibrates. Small air spaces vibrate more quickly than large spaces, making higher notes. So partly empty bottles produce lower notes than fuller ones.

Silent space

Sound can travel through solids, liquids, and gases, but it can't travel where there is no matter. There is no sound in space because there is no air.

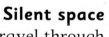

Sound waves travel through air like a wave along a coiled spring.

How hearing works

When a sound reaches your ears, it makes your eardrums vibrate. The vibrations are passed to your inner ear through tiny bones. From here, nerves send messages to your brain that allow you to recognize the sound.

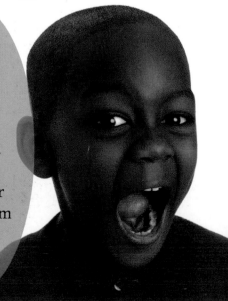

Measuring sound

Loudness is measured in decibels.

Rustling leaves make a sound of only 10 decibels.

Whispering measures about 20 decibels.

City traffic reaches approximately 85 decibels.

Drums make a sound of around 105 decibels.

Road-drills measure about 110 decibels.

A lion's roar has been recorded at 114 decibels.

Fireworks can measure 120 decibels or more.

Jet engines sometimes hit 140 decibels.

Do all animals hear the same sounds?

Speeding sound

All sounds travel at the same speed, but they travel more quickly through solids and liquids than through gases. Supersonic jets fly faster than the speed of sound, so they can pass over you before you hear their sound.

When a supersonic jet breaks the speed of sound, it catches up with the sound waves in front of it and squashes them. As the air is squashed, it produces a sound called a "sonic boom".

The echo effect

Some animals use sound to communicate or to hunt. Dolphins "talk" by making clicks, barks and other sounds that other dolphins recognize. They also use clicks to find food – the sound bounces back off objects as an echo, so the dolphin can establish their shape and position. This is called echolocation.

When sounds bounce back, the dolphin can tell if the object is a yummy fish or another dolphin!

241

No – dogs can hear higher notes than people, and squid can't hear at all.

Forces and motion

It can be difficult to make an object move, but once it is moving, it will go on moving until something stops it. Force is needed to start something moving, make it move faster, and make it stop.

The football would stay still if the footballer didn't kick it.

Newton's laws of motion

In 1687, Sir Isaac Newton worked out three important rules that explain how forces make things move. They have become the foundation of physics and work for just about everything, from footballs to frogs.

Newton's first law
An object stays still if it isn't being pushed or pulled by a force, or it keeps moving in a straight line at a constant speed.

Forces make things accelerate. The force is created by the cyclist's powerful legs.

Newton's second law
The bigger the force and the lighter the object, the greater the acceleration. A professional cyclist with a lightweight bike will accelerate faster than a normal person cycling to work.

Newton's third law
Every action has an equal and opposite reaction. The leaf moves away as the frog leaps in the opposite direction.

242

Speed and velocity

Speed is different to velocity. How quick you are going is easy to work out – divide how far you travel by the time it takes. Your velocity is how fast you travel in a particular direction. Changing direction without slowing reduces your velocity, but your speed stays the same.

Drive 80 km (50 miles) in two hours, speed is 40 kph (25 mph).

Accelerating is fun, but in science

The golf ball will carry on rolling until friction, gravity, and air resistance slow it down.

Rescue helicopters balance forces so they can hover above the waves.

LIFT

DRAG/ FRICTION

THRUST

GRAVITY

Inertia

When things are standing still or moving, they are quite happy to continue with what they are doing. This stubbornness is called inertia – it is the object's resistance to change.

Become an expert

234-235 What is energy?
244-245 Machines

Balanced forces

Forces act on objects all the time. Opposing forces can be balanced out. When this happens the object won't be pushed in any direction.

The maximum velocity of falling through air is 200 kph (124 mph).

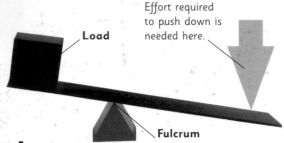

Load

Effort required to push down is needed here.

Fulcrum

Levers

A lever is a bar that swivels on a fixed point or fulcrum and makes it easier to move a load. When you move your end further (the effort), the load at the other end moves a short way powerfully.

One type of lever works like a see-saw with the fulcrum between the load and the effort.

Another type places the load between the fulcrum and the effort (as on a wheelbarrow).

A third type of lever, shown by tongs, places the effort between the fulcrum and the load.

Machines

Machines make tasks easier. They reduce the effort you need to move something, or the time it takes. They work either by spreading the load, or by concentrating your efforts.

Axle

Wheel and axle

An axle goes through the centre of a wheel. Together they work as a simple rotating machine that makes it easier to move something from one place to another.

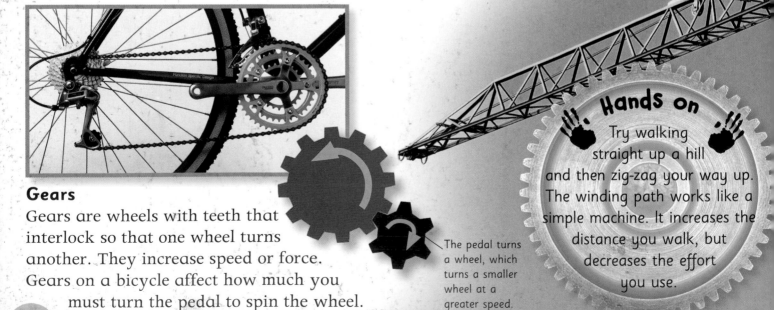

Gears

Gears are wheels with teeth that interlock so that one wheel turns another. They increase speed or force. Gears on a bicycle affect how much you must turn the pedal to spin the wheel.

The pedal turns a wheel, which turns a smaller wheel at a greater speed.

Hands on

Try walking straight up a hill and then zig-zag your way up. The winding path works like a simple machine. It increases the distance you walk, but decreases the effort you use.

Name six simple machines.

Wedge

An axe blade is an efficient but simple machine that increases force. When it hits the wood, the wedge forces the wood to split apart between its fibres.

It takes just one man to pull a stone up the slope, but four men are needed to lift a stone straight up.

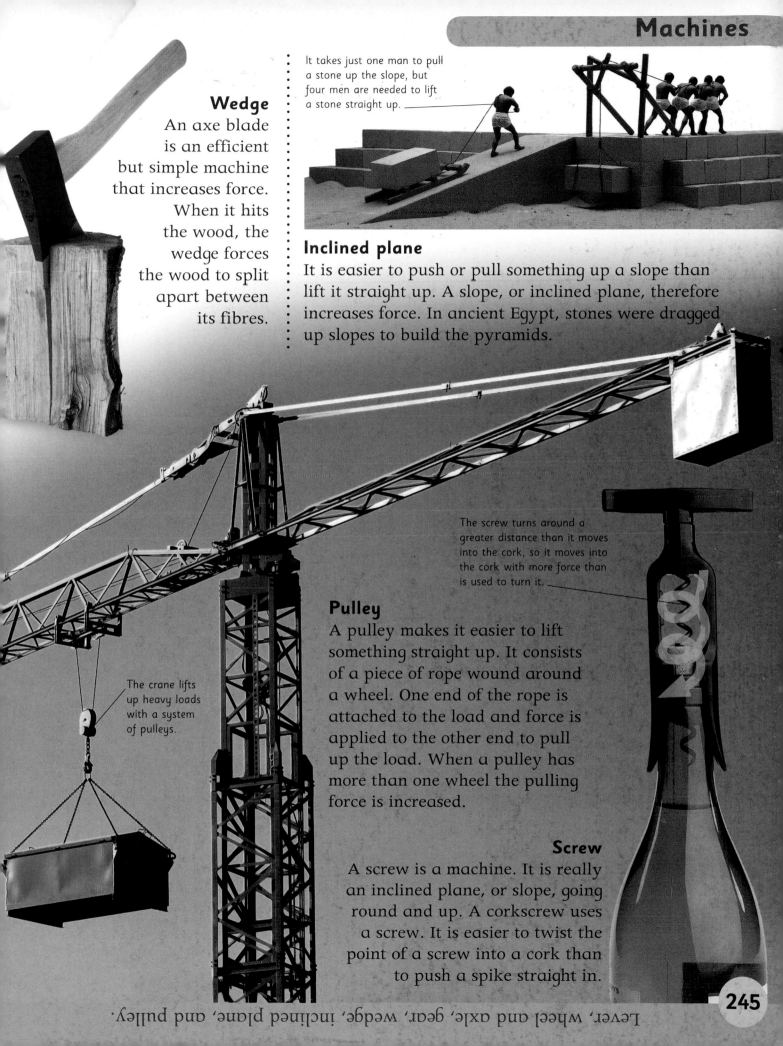

Inclined plane

It is easier to push or pull something up a slope than lift it straight up. A slope, or inclined plane, therefore increases force. In ancient Egypt, stones were dragged up slopes to build the pyramids.

The screw turns around a greater distance than it moves into the cork, so it moves into the cork with more force than is used to turn it.

The crane lifts up heavy loads with a system of pulleys.

Pulley

A pulley makes it easier to lift something straight up. It consists of a piece of rope wound around a wheel. One end of the rope is attached to the load and force is applied to the other end to pull up the load. When a pulley has more than one wheel the pulling force is increased.

Screw

A screw is a machine. It is really an inclined plane, or slope, going round and up. A corkscrew uses a screw. It is easier to twist the point of a screw into a cork than to push a spike straight in.

Lever, wheel and axle, gear, wedge, inclined plane, and pulley.

Our planet

The Earth is the planet where we all live. It is a huge ball of hot, liquid rock with a solid surface called the crust. Planet Earth travels in space.

The Earth's axis goes through its poles.

North Pole

The Earth's axis...

... is tilted to one side.

South Pole

Spinning Earth

The Earth slowly spins around once a day. The line it spins around is called the Earth's axis. At the ends of the axis are the Earth's poles.

The Earth's surface

There are seven huge pieces of land on the Earth's surface. They are called continents. They cover about one-third of the surface. Oceans cover the rest.

Earth as a magnet

Have you ever used a compass to find your way? It works because the Earth acts as if it has a giant bar magnet in the middle.

Which is the biggest ocean on the Earth?

What's it made of?

The Earth is made up of an outer thin crust. Under this is molten rock. In the middle is a solid core.

Curiosity quiz

Look through the Planet Earth pages and see if you can identify each of the picture clues below.

The crust

The Earth's crust is cracked into lots of huge pieces called plates. The cracks are called fault lines.

The San Andreas fault, California, USA

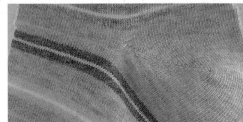

Mountains and valleys

Most mountains are made when rocks are pushed upwards by movements of the Earth's crust. Blowing winds, flowing rivers, and glaciers wear away the mountains.

Sedona, Arizona, south-western USA

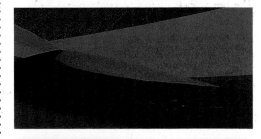

Become an expert

6-7 Our world
272-273 Our place in space

The Pacific Ocean. It covers nearly half of the Earth's surface.

Earth's structure

Earth is the only planet in the Solar System that can support life, because it's just the right distance from the Sun. Our amazing world is a huge ball of liquid rock with a solid surface.

Seen from space, Earth is a mass of blue oceans and swirling clouds.

Crust

Core

Outer core

Inside the Earth

If you could cut the Earth open, you'd see it's made up of layers. The thin top layer, where we live, is called the crust. Underneath is a layer of syrup-like rock called the mantle, then an outer core of molten (liquid) iron and nickel. At the centre is a solid iron-and-nickel core.

Life-support systems
Earth's atmosphere and its surface water play an important role in supporting life. They help keep our planet at just the right temperature by absorbing the Sun's heat and moving it around the world.

What is the world's tallest mountain range?

Volcanoes

Volcanoes are openings in the Earth's crust. Sometimes magma (melted rock) from just beneath the crust bursts through these openings as a volcanic eruption. Lots of ash and dust shoot out too.

Making mountains

The Himalayas started to form 50 million years ago, when two moving plates collided. The mountains are still growing!

Earthquakes often occur along the San Andreas Fault.

Fault lines

Earthquakes happen when "plates" rub against each other.

Drifting continents

The world hasn't always looked like it does now. Millions of years ago, all the land was joined together. Slowly, it broke up and the continents drifted apart.

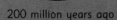

200 million years ago   135 million years ago   10 million years ago

Cracked crust

Earth's top layer is made up of giant pieces called "plates". These fit together a bit like a jigsaw, but they're constantly moving. Volcanoes and earthquakes often happen in the weak spots where plates move against each other.

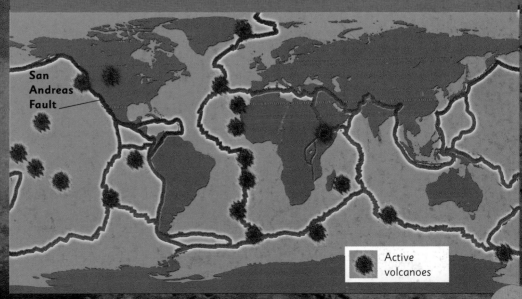

San Andreas Fault

Active volcanoes

The Himalayas.

Rocks and minerals

The Earth's crust is made up of different rocks. Some of these are hard but others are soft and crumbly. They are formed in different ways.

Serpentine is a mineral that stone carvers use to create works of art.

Gabbro is a rock that is used to make kitchen surfaces and floors.

White mica is a mineral that you can find in some kinds of toothpaste.

What is a rock?

A rock is formed from minerals. Most rocks are made up of different minerals, but some contain just one. There are three main types of rock: igneous, sedimentary, and metamorphic.

Fossils in stones
Fossils are the remains or imprints of plants and animals that died millions of years ago, preserved in stone.

The rock cycle

Over millions of years, the rocks in the Earth's crust can gradually change from one type into another. They are transformed by wind, water, pressure, and heat.

Igneous rock
Igneous rocks are made when hot molten magma from the Earth's interior cools and solidifies. Some harden underground like granite. Some erupt first as lava in a volcano.

Sedimentary rock
Wind and water wear rocks away. Small pieces, called sediments, wash into the sea. These settle into layers, which pack together to form sedimentary rocks, such as limestone and sandstone.

Metamorphic rock
Sometimes rocks are crushed underground, or scorched by hot magma. Then they may be transformed into new rocks such as marble, slate, and gneiss.

Which type of rock floats on water?

Rock salt is a mineral that is spread on roads in icy weather. It makes the ice melt.

What is a mineral?

A mineral is a solid that occurs naturally. It is made up of chemicals and has a crystal structure. Minerals are everywhere you look. We use minerals to build cars and computers, fertilize soil, and to clean our teeth.

Mineral mixtures

Granite rock is made up of different coloured minerals. The black mineral is mica, the pink is feldspar, and the grey mineral is quartz.

Feldspar is used for glazing ceramics.

Mica is ground up and used in paint.

Quartz can also occur as the gemstone amethyst.

Crystals

Minerals usually form crystals. Crystals have a number of flat surfaces. The largest crystals form when minerals in magma or trapped liquids cool very slowly.

Quartz stalactites form in caves over thousands of years.

Minerals in your home

Halite Salt is the mineral halite. We add it to our food for flavour.

Quartz from sand is used to make the silicon chips in calculators and computers.

Kaolinite is used to make crockery. It is also used to make paper look glossy.

Illite is a clay mineral and is used in terracotta pots and bricks.

Mica is used to make glittery paint and nail polish.

Graphite is the "lead" in pencils. It is also used in bicycle brakes.

Rhodochrosite is a rose-coloured gemstone used in jewellery.

Pumice is filled with air bubbles, so some pieces can float.

Shaping the land

The surface of our planet never stops changing. Over millions of years, land is slowly worn away by wind, rain, and rivers. Floods, volcanoes, and earthquakes can change the shape of the land in just a few hours.

River power
The Grand Canyon formed over millions of years as the Colorado River slowly wore ever deeper into the rock.

Going underground
Caves form when rain seeps underground and eats away at soft rock such as limestone.

Coastal shapes
Powerful waves shape the coastlines around the world's oceans.

Bays form where waves wear into areas of softer rock along the coast.

Headlands are areas of harder rock that have not been worn away.

Sea arches form when waves open up cracks in headlands.

Sea stacks are pillars of rock left in the sea after an arch collapses.

Glaciers at work
Glaciers are huge rivers of ice that flow slowly off snowcapped mountains. Broken rock sticks to the bottom of the glacier, which then wears away the land like sandpaper, carving out a deep, U-shaped valley.

What is the most active volcano on Earth?

New islands

Some volcanoes are hidden under the sea. When they erupt, they can give birth to whole new islands, like Surtsey in Iceland (left). Surtsey burst out of the sea in 1963.

Before flood

After flood

Floods

Heavy rain makes rivers overflow, causing floods. Floods have enormous power and can wreck buildings and re-shape the land.

Hills of sand

In deserts, winds blow sand into hills called dunes. In some deserts the dunes stretch for hundreds of miles, forming a "sand sea".

Worn by wind

Strong winds can lift sand off the ground and blast it hard against rocks. The rock is worn into strange shapes.

Mount Kilauea in Hawaii.

253

Soil

Soil is the thin layer of loose material on the land. Soil contains minerals, air, water, and decaying organic matter.

Layers in soil

Soil builds up in layers over many years. Plant roots grow in the topsoil, which is generally the richest in plant food. The lower layers are rocky. Plant roots do not reach this far down in the soil.

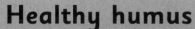

Humus

Topsoil

Subsoil

Regolith

Bedrock

Healthy humus

Humus is a dark, rich substance made up of rotting plants and animals (called "organic matter"). It contains lots of nutrients, which plants need to grow.

Life underground

Soil is home to thousands of animals, including slugs, ants, beetles, and spiders. Larger animals that spend time underground, such as moles, mix up humus and minerals as they burrow through the soil.

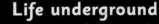

What is a scientist who studies soil called?

Sizing up soil

Different types of soil have different sized particles.

Sandy soils contain particles about 2 mm (0.08 in) across.

Clay soils have very small particles. Water collects between them.

Loamy soils have a mixture of small and large particles.

Soil erosion

When soil is farmed too much, its nutrients get used up. The topsoil blows or washes away. Not many plants can survive in these areas without the rich topsoil.

Ploughing helps keep soil fertile.

Ploughing breaks up soil to stop it getting hard and solid. This helps crops grow more easily.

Important earthworms

Earthworms help to make fertile soil. Their burrows let air into the soil, and create pathways for water to move around more easily. Earthworms also help the remains of plants and animals to decompose. This releases important nutrients into the soil. Earthworm waste is good for soil too!

Hands on

Half fill a jar with soil and top it up with water. Put on the lid and shake. Leave for a day. The soil should separate into layers.

A pedologist.

Resources in the ground

The ground holds many useful things, from fuels like coal and oil, to drinking water, and building materials. These valuable items are known as resources and we have dug, drilled, and searched for them for many years.

Sea level — **Rig**

People drill holes to extract oil and gas from deep under the sea floor.

Finding fuels

Oil and gas are often found in pockets deep underground. Sometimes, these are even below the seabed. Coal develops closer to the surface in layers called seams.

Deep drilling

Oil rigs far out at sea use huge drills to extract the liquid oil from the ground. Coal is solid and is dug out in mines or pits.

In hot water

Water in the ground can get very hot near volcanoes. In Iceland, they use this naturally hot water to heat houses or make steam to turn electricity generators.

Which underground resource are plastics made from?

Getting gas
Gas is only found in certain places. To get it to where it is needed, it is fed through very long pipes, or changed into liquid and put in special ships.

Making glass
Glass is made by melting together sand, soda ash, and ground limestone. People blow or machine press the red-hot mineral mixture into different shapes that set hard and clear as the glass cools.

Glass bottles are shaped from molten glass.

Extracting metals
Most metals are found underground as minerals in rocks called ores. Giant machines dig up the ore. The metal is extracted, or taken out, from the ore using heat.

Metal variety
Different metal resources have different uses.

Aluminium is a soft metal used to make cans, aircraft, and car bodies.

Gold is rare and looks attractive, so it is often used to make jewellery.

Iron is strong. It is used to make steel for ships, buildings, and pylons.

Copper conducts electricity and is used to make electrical wires.

Creating concrete
Concrete is an important building material. It is a mixture of sand, gravel, cement, and water. All these ingredients are found in the ground.

Oil.

Fresh and salt water

Earth is often called the blue planet because 75 per cent of its surface is covered in water. Most of the Earth's water is salt water in the oceans. Less than one per cent of all the water on Earth is fresh.

The hydrosphere

The hydrosphere is the name for all the water on Earth. It includes oceans, rivers, and lakes. It also includes water that is frozen, such as icebergs.

Freshwater sources

People get fresh water from different sources on Earth's surface, including rivers, streams, lakes, and reservoirs.

Rivers and streams flow from mountains down to the oceans.

Lakes are natural dips in the Earth where water collects.

Reservoirs are man-made lakes that are built to store water.

Trapped in ice

Less than 33 per cent of fresh water is usable by humans. The rest is frozen in glaciers or icebergs (below), or as huge sheets of ice at the North and South poles.

Water for life
All animals – and most other living things – must have water to survive. In mammals, including humans, water is part of the blood and of organs such as the skin and brain. There is water in every cell in your body!

How much of your body is water?

Salty seas

The world's oceans are salty because they contain a lot of dissolved chemicals that scientists call salts. Drinking water also contains salts, but only in small amounts, so you can't taste them.

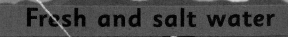

The Dead Sea contains so much salt that people can just float on the surface.

Surviving in salt water

Countless animals live in water. They don't drink, but take water into their bodies in other ways. Fish often absorb water as it washes in and out of their gills. Salt-water fish absorb only a little of the salt.

Hands on

Put an egg in a glass of water. The egg will sink. Start stirring in salt until the egg rises. The egg will eventually float because salt water is denser than fresh water.

Estuary life

An estuary is the wide part of a river where it nears the sea. When the tide comes in, salt water flows into the estuary. When the tide goes out, the estuary contains mostly fresh water from the river or stream that flows into it. Mangrove trees like these are able to live in the changing estuary water.

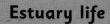

Your body is approximately 66 per cent water.

The water cycle

Water is constantly on the move, between oceans, land, air, and rivers. This movement is called the water cycle.

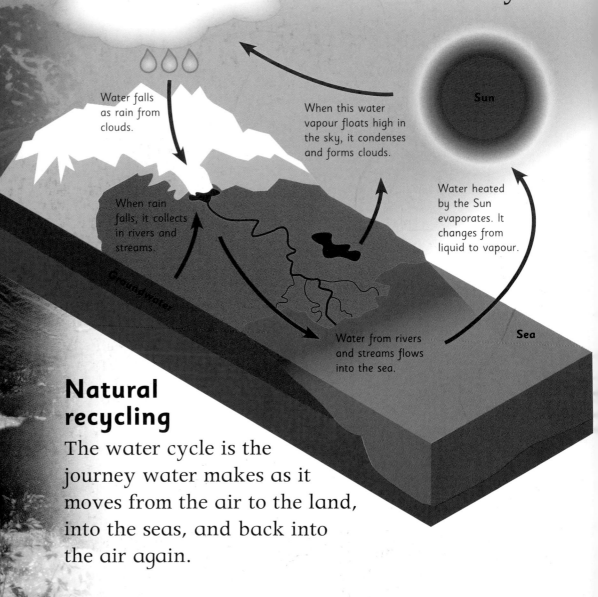

Water falls as rain from clouds.

When this water vapour floats high in the sky, it condenses and forms clouds.

Sun

When rain falls, it collects in rivers and streams.

Water heated by the Sun evaporates. It changes from liquid to vapour.

Groundwater

Water from rivers and streams flows into the sea.

Sea

Natural recycling

The water cycle is the journey water makes as it moves from the air to the land, into the seas, and back into the air again.

On the dry side

Moisture-laden sea air has to rise when it hits a coastal mountain. Since air cools as it rises, all the moisture condenses into rain. So, on the other side of the mountain, no rain falls – this area is called a rainshadow.

What is electricity generated by running water called?

Groundwater

In the water cycle, some water seeps underground, where it collects in rocks and sometimes forms pools in caves. Some groundwater is pumped up and used for drinking or irrigation.

Using water

Fresh water is trapped in reservoirs and then piped to homes, businesses, and farms. When you turn on a tap, the water that comes out has been on a long journey!

Damp ground

Wetlands form on land in areas where fresh water does not drain away. They provide a home for many water-loving plants, birds, animals, and fish.

Saving water

There is a limited amount of fresh water on Earth. If we want to make sure there's enough to go around, it's important that everyone uses less.

Drought

When very little rain falls, experts call this a drought. Droughts do not occur only in deserts – any area that gets much less rain than usual is said to be suffering from drought.

Turn off taps when you finish brushing your teeth or washing.

Flush the toilet only when necessary. Some toilets have two flush controls.

Don't run the dishwasher when it's half empty – wait until it's full.

Take a shower instead of a bath. Showering uses much less water.

Hydroelectricity.

The atmosphere

Planet Earth is wrapped in a thin layer of air called the atmosphere. Without this protective blanket of gases, life on Earth could not exist.

Gases in air

Air is a mixture of different gases, including nitrogen, oxygen, and carbon dioxide. Oxygen is vital for plants and animals as it allows them to breathe. Carbon dioxide is vital for plants. They absorb it from the air and use the carbon atoms to help build new leaves and stems.

Shimmering particles
The atmosphere is mainly made up of gases, but it also contains tiny particles of dust, pollen, and water droplets. All particles can cause a haze in the air when the Sun shines through them.

The greenhouse effect
If there was no atmosphere, the Sun's warming rays would bounce off Earth and disappear into space. But the atmosphere traps some of the heat, making Earth warm enough for us to survive.

From space, the atmosphere looks like a blue haze over Earth.

Protective layer
A gas called ozone in the atmosphere protects Earth from harmful rays in sunlight. Above Antarctica there is an area of the ozone layer that is much thinner than anywhere else. This "ozone hole" was caused by chemical pollution.

How far up from the ground does space officially begin?

Into thin air

Like everything else, air is pulled by gravity. Most air molecules are pulled close to the ground, where the air is thick and easy to breathe. Higher up, air is so thin that climbers need oxygen tanks.

Layers of the atmosphere

The atmosphere is made up of layers, each with a different name. The bottom layer is the troposphere, where clouds form and planes fly. Above this, the air gets thinner and thinner as the atmosphere merges into space.

Light spectacular

Sunlight can create dazzling effects as it strikes the atmosphere and is scattered by air, water, and dust.

 Rainbows form when water droplets reflect sunlight and split it into different colours.

 The sky looks blue on clear days because air molecules scatter blue light the most.

 At sunset and sunrise, dust and hazy cloud in the air turn the sky orange and red.

Moving water

The atmosphere is always swirling around, creating winds. The winds push on the oceans, causing the water to swirl too. These swirling currents carry warmth around the planet.

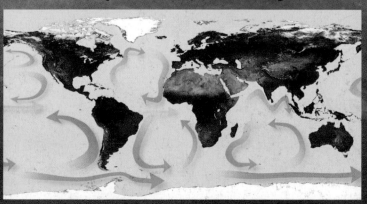

THERMOSPHERE

500 km (310 miles)

Satellite

Space shuttle

Northern lights

MESOSPHERE

85 km (53 miles)
Shooting stars

STRATOSPHERE

50 km (31 miles)

Weather balloon

TROPOSPHERE

10 km (6 miles)

Jumbo jet

Weather

Is it sunny or rainy? Is there snow on the ground or a thunderstorm brewing? People are always interested in the weather because it affects what we do and what we wear.

Kites stay high in the air by catching the wind.

Weather words

Here are some main features of the weather.

Sunshine gives us heat and light. It warms the air and dries the land.

Clouds are made from tiny water droplets. Dark clouds mean rain is coming.

Hailstones are balls of ice that grow inside thunderclouds.

Wind is air moving around. Winds can be a light breeze or a strong gale.

Rain is drops of water that fall from clouds. Rain is very good for plant life.

Snow is made from tiny bits of ice. It falls instead of rain when it is very cold.

Predicting the weather

Weather forecasters look at pictures beamed back from weather satellites. Computers then help forecasters work out what the weather is going to be like over the next few days.

Rainy days

Rain clouds form when warm, moist air rises upwards and then cools. Droplets of water join together until they become so heavy that they fall. Rain clouds look dark because sunlight cannot shine through the droplets.

Which is bigger: a tornado or a hurricane?

Wildfires

Long periods of hot or dry weather can make plants dry out so much that they catch fire easily when struck by lightning. This can lead to a raging wildfire that burns down whole forests.

Stormy weather

Lightning strikes when electricity builds up in clouds. The electricity is created when ice crystals in the clouds rub against each other. A bolt of lightning heats the air around it so quickly that the air explodes, creating the rumbling noise we call thunder.

The brightest bolts of lightning travel upwards from the ground to the clouds.

Winds on the move

Wind is moving air. Warm air rises and cool air sinks. This movement is what makes the wind blow.

Twisters

Tornadoes (twisters) are whirling funnels of wind that form beneath massive thunderclouds. The fierce wind can do enormous damage, and the funnel can suck up debris like a gigantic vacuum cleaner.

weird or what?

In certain conditions hailstones can grow to be enormous. The biggest ever hailstone weighed 1 kg (2 lb) and was over 40 cm (16 in) across!

A hurricane is thousands of times bigger than a tornado.

The energy crisis

People around the world use energy for many different purposes – from powering cars, to heating homes. Most of this energy comes from burning coal, oil, and natural gas (fossil fuels). But these fuels won't last forever, and their fumes are damaging the atmosphere.

Nuclear power stations generate energy by splitting atoms.

Global warming

Burning fossil fuels fills the air with greenhouse gases, which trap some of the Sun's heat in the atmosphere. If Earth becomes too warm, deserts will spread, icebergs will melt, and sea levels will rise.

Alternative energy

We need to find sources of energy other than fossil fuels – sources that cause less pollution and will not run out. Nuclear power is one option. Others possibilities include energy from sunlight, wind, and waves.

Heat from the Sun enters through the atmosphere.

Greenhouse gases trap heat, although some escapes back into the atmosphere.

The wind provides a limitless supply of non-polluting energy. However, wind turbines are large and can be costly to set up.

What are fossil fuels made of?

Cleaner cars

Ordinary petrol cars use a lot of oil, and produce harmful fumes. Now car makers are looking for alternatives to petrol. Electric cars do not give off any kind of fumes. Hydrogen engines burn hydrogen gas, and only give off water.

To recharge an electric car, you just plug it in.

Making a difference

There are lots of small things we can all do to save energy.

Start growing your own vegetables and fruit, even if they're only in pots.

When planning a holiday, remember that trains, boats, and cars use less energy than aeroplanes.

Instead of buying new clothes, swap with a friend or buy them second-hand.

Eat local food that hasn't travelled miles, because transporting food costs energy.

Don't throw away glass, plastics, metal, or paper – reuse or recycle them.

Take your own bags when you go shopping. Making plastic bags takes energy.

Don't leave your TV or DVD on standby – this wastes lots of electricity.

Hang your laundry outside to dry. Don't waste electricity running a dryer.

Ask your parents about insulating the roof to prevent heat from escaping.

If you get cold, put on a jumper instead of turning up your heating.

Rising energy needs

As the world's population grows, we are using more and more energy. But to stop global warming, we may have to reduce the amount of energy we all use.

Energy-saving homes

This house saves energy by using solar panels and wind turbines to generate its own non-polluting electricity. The walls are thick, so that less energy is needed to heat the house.

To reduce the energy used in manufacturing, it's a good idea to use recycled building materials.

The remains of plants and animals that lived millions of years ago.

Where does space begin?

Earth is cloaked in a thin layer of gases – the atmosphere. Outside this atmosphere is space, where there is no air to breathe, or to allow wings to fly, and where nobody can hear you scream.

Fading away

Our atmosphere does not just end suddenly – it fades gradually into space.

View from *Mir*

Photographed from the American shuttle *Atlantis*, the Russian *Mir* space station once orbited above Earth's atmosphere.

EXOSPHERE

THERMOSPHERE

MESOSPHERE

STRATOSPHERE

TROPOSPHERE

The **exosphere** is the outer layer of the atmosphere, extending about 10,000 km (6,000 miles) above the ground. From here, lighter gases drift into space beyond.

The **thermosphere** reaches way up to more than 700 km (over 400 miles) above Earth. The polar lights (*aurora borealis* in the north and *aurora australis* in the south) glow in the thermosphere.

Most experts agree that space begins at 100 km (62 miles) above the ground. Past this, our image is not drawn to scale.

In turn, the **mesosphere** extends about 85 km (53 miles) above the ground. The air is thin here, but it's still thick enough to slow meteorites down.

The **stratosphere** rises about 50 km (31 miles) above the Earth. Planes cruise in the upper troposphere or lower stratosphere, above the clouds.

The **troposphere** extends between 6 and 20 km (3½–12 miles) above the ground. All our weather takes place in the troposphere.

What do we call the mix of gases that makes up our atmosphere?

Space badge

The American space agency NASA awards astronaut wings to service personnel and civilians who have flown more than 80 km (50 miles) above the Earth's surface. Shown here are civilian astronaut wings.

If you could drive a car straight up, it would take only about an hour to reach space.

Gaia, a European satellite due for launch in 2011.

Slipping through air

A spacecraft has to be streamlined to move easily and safely through air. Where necessary, an extra part called a fairing is added to achieve this effect — a nose cone is a fairing.

The parts of a space shuttle (the orbiter, fuel tank, and rocket boosters) are streamlined for lift-off.

Space hat-ellite

Satellites can be any shape at all — even hat shaped. They don't need to be streamlined, because there's no air in space.

271

Our place in space

Earth seems huge to us – after all, it can take you a long time just to travel to school! But Earth is only a very tiny part of space. So where exactly does it belong in the Universe?

Earth looks like a swirly blue marble suspended in space.

The Earth and its moon

Earth, our home in space, has one natural satellite, our moon. The moon is about one quarter the size of Earth and, on average, it orbits about 384,000 km (240,000 miles) from us.

Uranus

Mars

Venus

Saturn

Mercury

Earth

Jupiter

Neptune

This picture shows where the planets are located. None of them, or their orbits, are drawn to scale.

Astronauts who have seen Earth from space are struck by its beauty. One described it as looking like a Christmas-tree decoration.

The solar system

Earth is the third planet from the Sun, at just the right distance from it to support life. The eight planets that orbit the Sun (plus moons, comets, asteroids, meteors, dwarf planets, dust, and gas) make up our solar system.

There used to be a ninth planet, Pluto, but this is now classed as a dwarf planet.

In a spin
Our galaxy has long curved arms that spiral out from a central bulge.

The Milky Way

Our Sun

The Local Group
The Milky Way is one of the largest galaxies in a cluster known as the Local Group. Millions of galaxy clusters make up the Universe.

The Milky Way
Our solar system is located in a galaxy called the Milky Way, a collection of billions of stars. It lies on the edge of one of the spiral arms.

Our home in space supports trillions of living things.

The Milky Way

Our solar system is a tiny – tiny! – part of a gigantic spiral galaxy, the Milky Way. This is made up of billions of stars, which look as if they have been sprinkled thickly onto the night sky.

Scientists think there are about 100,000 million stars in the Milky Way galaxy, but there may be even more.

Why is it milky?

Before the invention of telescopes, people could not see the stars very clearly – they were blurred together in a hazy white streak. The ancient Greeks called this streak a "river of milk". This is how our galaxy became known as the Milky Way.

Milky myths

Many myths have developed about the formation of the Milky Way.

Become an expert

272-273 Our place in space

290-291 A star is born

Native American stories tell of a dog dropping corn as he fled across the sky.

Kalahari bushmen say it was created by hot embers thrown up from a fire.

Hindu myth sees the milkiness as the speckled belly of a dolphin.

The ancient Egyptians believed the stars were a pool of cow's milk.

A side view
The Milky Way, like all spiral galaxies, is flat, with a bulge at the centre, and arms that circle outwards.

Where are the oldest stars in the Milky Way?

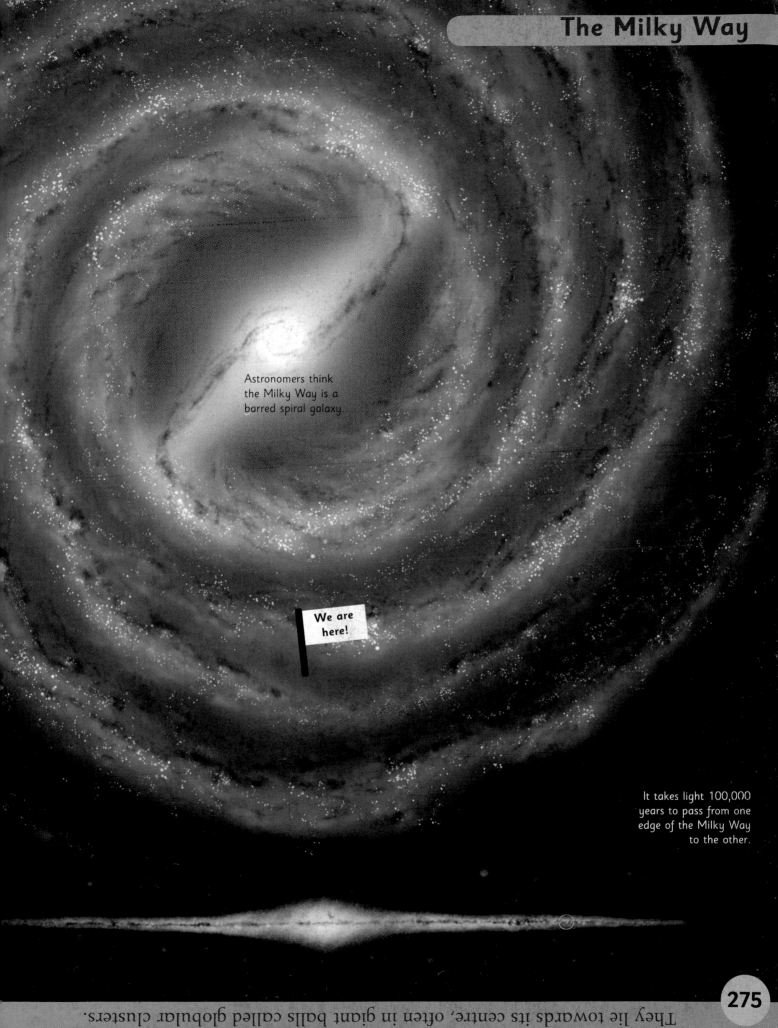

Astronomers think
the Milky Way is a
barred spiral galaxy.

We are
here!

It takes light 100,000
years to pass from one
edge of the Milky Way
to the other.

They lie towards its centre, often in giant balls called globular clusters.

Rockets

Rockets carry satellites and people into space. A rocket burns fuel to produce a jet of gas. The hot gas expands rapidly and is blasted downwards causing a force (the thrust) to push the rocket up.

A nose cone, or fairing, reduces air resistance as the rocket takes off.

Birth of the rocket

The first liquid-fuelled rocket was launched in 1926 by an American, Robert Goddard. It reached 12.5 m (41 ft). The flight lasted 2.5 seconds.

Vostok 1 spaceship

Launch of the *Long March 2C* rocket from the Jiuquan Space Centre, China, on August 19, 1983. Its main cargo was a photographic imaging satellite.

Long March 2C was 35.1 m (115 ft) long and 3.3 m (11 ft) wide.

First in space

The first person in space was the Russian cosmonaut, Yuri Gagarin. He was sent up in *Vostok 1* on April 12, 1961 for a 108-minute flight.

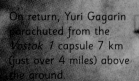

On return, Yuri Gagarin parachuted from the *Vostok 1* capsule 7 km (just over 4 miles) above the ground.

How many tests were needed for the engine that powered the first stage of *Ariane 5*?

To escape Earth's gravity, a rocket has to reach just over 11 km (7 miles) per second. This is called the escape velocity.

Ariane 5

Types of rocket
There are many different kinds of rocket.

Reusable space shuttles carry people to and from the space station.

Saturn V were the largest rockets ever built. They were used to launch all the moon landings.

Firework rockets are used for celebrations.

Military rockets have been used for hundreds of years.

Experimental rockets provide information about fast and high flight.

Some satellites have small rocket engines to position them once they are in orbit.

Regular launches
Today, rockets such as *Ariane 5* are used to launch satellites into space. A satellite is a rocket's payload, or cargo, whose size determines whether it is sent up by a small or large rocket.

Ariane 5 launch vehicle. The main tank contains 25 tonnes (27.5 tons) of liquid hydrogen. The tubes on each side are solid fuel boosters that supply extra power for lift-off.

Biggest and best
The *Saturn V* were the largest, and most powerful, rockets ever built. They were used 13 times, between 1968 and 1972, including for the first moon landing.

Around 300 tests were done.

Moon journey

During the 1960s there was a race between the USA and the former Soviet Union to put a man on the moon. The USA landed the first man on the moon with *Apollo 11* in 1969.

Apollo 11 reached the moon because of a huge rocket called *Saturn V*. Most of *Saturn V* contained the fuel needed to blast it into space. Three astronauts sat in a tiny capsule at the top of the rocket.

10 The service module is ejected before re-entry into Earth's atmosphere.

9

The journey back

11 The command module is the only part of the mission to return to Earth.

1 Five F1 engines blast the *Saturn V* rocket into space from the Kennedy Space Center.

The journey out

12

Command module

13

Earth

3 The command and service modules separate from the rocket and perform a 180° turn.

2 The rocket's engines fire to set the craft on a course to the moon.

The service module contained the power and life-support systems.

What was *Apollo 11*?
Apollo 11 was made up of three modules, or parts: the tiny command module, the service module, and the lunar module.

How many astronauts have walked on the moon?

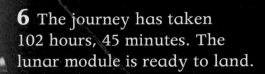

Become an expert

280-281 Men on the moon

276-277 Rockets,

6 The journey has taken 102 hours, 45 minutes. The lunar module is ready to land.

5 The rest of the rocket is discarded while the command, service, and lunar modules continue to the moon.

7 The command and service modules orbit the moon (one astronaut remains on board) while the lunar module lands. Two astronauts walk on the moon.

8 The lunar module joins the command and service modules so the two lunar astronauts can climb through. The lunar module is then abandoned.

4 The command and service modules reattach to the lunar module, which is still connected to the rocket.

The Eagle has landed

The lunar module (the part of *Apollo 11* that landed) was also known as the *Eagle*. It touched down on the surface of the moon on 20 July, 1969.

The three astronauts worked and slept in the command module.

Apollo 11

Mission commander Neil Armstrong struggled to find a flat landing site. He succeeded with just seconds to spare.

Men on the moon

On 20 July 1969, Neil Armstrong became the first person to walk on the surface of the moon. He was joined by Buzz Aldrin. A third astronaut, Mike Collins, remained in orbit with the command and service modules.

weird or what? The lunar module computer on *Apollo 11* had just 71K of memory. Some calculators can now store more than 500K.

The lunar module was nicknamed the *Eagle*.

What did they do?
Armstrong and Aldrin spent almost 22 hours on the moon. About 2.5 hours of this was spent outside the *Eagle*, collecting rock and soil samples, setting up experiments, and taking pictures.

What was it like?
Buzz Aldrin described the moon's surface as like nothing on Earth. He said it consisted of a fine, talcum-powder-like dust, strewn with pebbles and rocks.

Why is there no blue sky on the moon?

Here comes Earth

Instead of the moon rising, the astronauts saw Earth rising over the moon's horizon – it looked four times bigger than the moon looks from Earth.

How did they talk?

There's no air in space, so sound has nothing to travel through. Lunar astronauts use radio equipment in their helmets.

Neil Armstrong

We have transport!

Three later *Apollo* missions each carried a small electric car, a lunar rover, which allowed the astronauts to explore away from the lander. These were left on the moon when the astronauts left.

This dish antennae allowed the astronauts to send pictures to Earth.

One lunar rover reached a top speed of 22 km/h (13.5 mph).

Splashdown

The astronauts returned to Earth in the *Apollo 11* command module. This fell through the atmosphere and landed in the Pacific Ocean. A ringed float helped to keep it stable.

Because the moon has no atmosphere.

Space shuttle

A partly reusable craft built by the US to send astronauts into space, the shuttle was first launched in April 1981.

Which bit is that?

The shuttle has three main components: the orbiter (the plane part, and the only part that goes into orbit), a huge fuel tank, and two rocket boosters.

Heat protection
Nearly 25,000 heat-resistant tiles cover the orbiter to protect it from high temperatures on re-entry.

Ditch the tanks!
The rocket boosters are released two minutes after launch. They parachute back to Earth and will be used again. The tank is discarded eight minutes after launch, and breaks up in the atmosphere.

Main (external) fuel tank

The orbiter carries between five and seven crew members.

There are two rocket boosters, one on each side. Once lit, the boosters cannot be shut off; they burn until they run out of fuel.

The orbiter's engines are used once the orbiter reaches space.

weird or what?

Woodpeckers delayed a space shuttle launch in 1995 by pecking holes in the fuel tank's insulating foam. Plastic owls are now used to frighten other birds away.

How long does it take the orbiter to reach space?

Pop it in there!

Each orbiter has a huge payload bay. You could park a school bus in this cavity, which holds the satellites, experiments, and laboratories that need to be taken into space.

The payload's doors open once the shuttle is in orbit.

The orbiter fleet

Five orbiters were built. Two have been lost in tragic accidents.

 Columbia first flew in 1981. It disintegrated on re-entry in 2003.

 Challenger was destroyed in 1986, just 73 seconds after launch.

 Discovery first flew in 1984. It marked the 100th shuttle mission in 2000.

 Atlantis first flew in 1985. It has completed more than 25 missions.

 Endeavour was built to replace *Challenger*. It first flew in 1992.

Space shuttle *Endeavour* landing at Edwards Air Force Base, California, USA.

A safe landing

Shuttles glide down, belly first. Once the orbiter touches the runway, it releases a 12 m (40 ft) drag chute to slow it down.

The future shuttle

NASA are currently working on designs for a new orbiter, the *Orion* Crew Exploration Vehicle (CEV). It will travel into space on an *Ares 1* rocket launcher, and carry up to six astronauts on each mission.

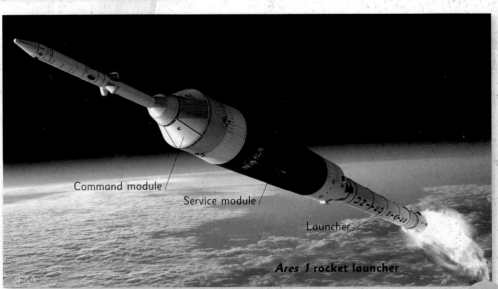

Command module

Service module

Launcher

Ares 1 rocket launcher

It takes just over eight minutes.

Working in space

The International Space Station (ISS) seen from the space shuttle *Discovery*.

We have all seen workers on a construction site, hammering and drilling. Imagine a construction site floating in space high above the Earth's surface. That's what astronauts have to cope with when they are repairing a satellite, or putting together a space station.

Is it warm today?

In orbit, the strong sunshine heats astronauts up. Surprisingly, it's difficult to lose heat in space, so spacesuits have to include a refrigeration unit!

Illustration of how a sunrise would look from space.

An astronaut may be outside the space station for hours at a time. This one is working on the station's robotic arm.

Between 1998 and 2005, more than 60 spacewalks were performed. Each time two astronauts worked on the International Space Station.

Hands on

Astronauts say that moving their hands in their gloves is difficult. To feel what they mean, put a rubber band around your closed fingers and try to open them. Do this fifteen times.

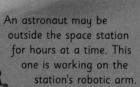

What does EVA stand for?

A piece of history

The first ever spacewalk was performed by Soviet astronaut Alexei Leonov on March 18th, 1965. He was soon followed by American Edward White on June 3rd, 1965.

Edward White was the first American to spacewalk.

Alexei Leonov became a celebrity in the Soviet Union and around the world.

Slow down

Astronauts have to work slower than construction workers on Earth. If they twist a bolt too quickly, they will send themselves into a spin.

Make it larger

Space tools are extra large so that astronauts can grab them in their bulky gloves. They also have to be tied to the astronaut to prevent them from floating away.

285

ExtraVehicular Activity. It means space walking!

Exploring Mars

Spacecraft have flown past Mars, orbited it, and landed on its surface. One day, we may even build a base on Mars. It may be cold, barren, and dusty, but it's full of possibilities.

Why study Mars?

At some point in its history, life may have existed on Mars. Although it's about half the size of Earth, it has clouds, weather patterns, and polar icecaps – once it even had active volcanoes. Learning about Mars may help us to understand our own planet.

Looking at Mars

There have been a number of missions to Mars.

In 1971, two spacecraft, *Mars 2* and *Mars 3*, got to Mars, but their landers failed to operate.

In 1976, two spacecraft, the *Viking* landers, tested for signs of life.

In 1996, *Mars Global Surveyor* was launched. It completed its first mission, but later lost contact.

In 1997, *Pathfinder* touched down, releasing a small rover called *Sojourner*.

In 1999, the *Mars Polar Lander* proved unsuccessful.

On the barren surface of Mars, the robotic *Sojourner* rover examines a rock later nicknamed "Yogi".

Seeing red

The landing craft that visited Mars took lots of pictures of its surface. These show a layer of soil that is rich in iron, which gives Mars its red colour – like rusty iron on Earth.

How much did it cost to build, launch, and land the Mars rovers?

What's happening now?

Two rovers, *Spirit* and *Opportunity*, have been exploring the Martian surface since 2004. They have sent back a wealth of data about the planet's surface, including plenty of evidence that there was once water on Mars.

Cameras mounted on masts give scientists panoramic views of the Martian surface.

Nasa rover *Spirit*

The rover is powered by solar panels.

This image shows a 9 mm (.35 in) hole in Mars' surface drilled and photographed by *Spirit*.

The future on Mars

Scientists are always searching for ways to unlock the secrets of the red planet. Among the ideas suggested are an aeroplane that could travel across its surface (above left) and a thermal probe that would penetrate its ice caps (above right).

In order to explore the potential of a colony in space, eight scientists lived in a self-contained dome, *Biosphere II*, for two years during the early 1990s.

Living on Mars

If we do establish a base on Mars, it will have to be a self-contained structure that protects its inhabitants from both the atmosphere and the Sun's radiation. Below is an artist's impression of what a Martian base might look like.

Approximately US $800 million.

The Sun

The Sun is white. Its colour is best seen when reflected in water. Never look directly at the Sun.

Our Sun is a star, but it is closer to us than any other star. Like all stars, it is a massive ball of burning gas, fed by constant explosions. Without it, our planet would be lifeless.

Shimmering lights can light up the skies towards the Earth's polar regions.

Solar wind

The Sun sends out a stream of invisible particles, called the solar wind. When these pass Earth's North and South Poles, they can create stunning colours.

Investigating the Sun

Various space probes have been designed to study the Sun.

Ulysses was launched in 1990 to look at the Sun's polar regions.

SOHO was launched in 1995 to observe the Sun and solar activity.

TRACE was launched in 1998 to study the Sun's atmosphere.

Long lived

The Sun was born just under five billion years ago. Although it burns four million tonnes (tons) of fuel each second, it is so big that it will continue to burn for another five billion years.

A hot spot?

White areas show places where the Sun's surface temperature is higher than elsewhere. Cooler, dark areas, called sunspots, sometimes appear on the surface.

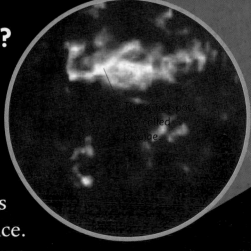

These hotspots are called foxulae

Does the Sun spin?

The size of
Earth compared
to the Sun.

The Sun is white, but
false colour images such
as this allow astronomers
to identify different
features on its surface.

It takes the Sun's heat about eight minutes to reach Earth.

Solar flares

Blasts of hot gas sometimes flare
up from the Sun's surface in
huge arcs or loops. They reach
thousands of kilometres (miles)
into space.

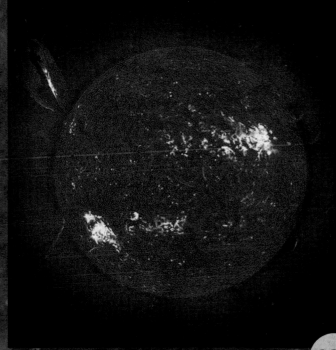

Yes, it does. It spins on its axis, like the planets of the solar system.

A star is born

Clusters of stars are constantly being born from clouds of dust and gas thousands of times the size of our solar system, in a process that can take millions of years.

Like many space pictures, this image of the Eagle nebula has been artificially coloured so it can be seen clearly.

Born in a cloud

Between existing stars, there are patches of dust and gas. Gradually, these draw in more and more dust and gas to form huge clouds called nebulae. Clumps of matter gather together in these clouds.

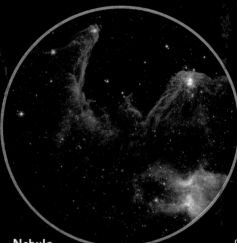

Nebula

Hot colours

As this matter gets more and more dense, heat builds up to form a young star that fills the surrounding nebulae with light and colour. This spectacular effect (right) was captured by the *Spitzer* space telescope.

The process of star formation captured by the *Hubble* telescope.

With enough matter, this process continues. The star gets denser and hotter. Eventually nuclear fusion begins, releasing huge amounts of heat and light: a star is born.

Which star cluster is also called the Seven Sisters?

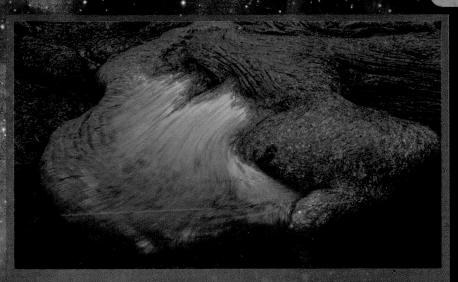

Is that one red?

Some stars shine red, others shine yellow or bluish white. A star's colour depends on its temperature. Red stars are the coolest, while blue stars are the hottest.

In the same way, lava reveals its temperature through its colour. Here, the yellow lava is hotter than the red

Our Sun is a yellow dwarf star.

What's in a name?

Horsehead, Lagoon, Eagle and Cat's Eye... some of the best-known nebulae have popular names inspired by their shape.

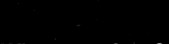

Cat's Eye nebula

What type of star?

Stars have different characteristics according to the amount of matter involved in their birth. They differ in colour, temperature, and brightness, and in the length of time they stay alive.

The life of a star

The Universe is home to lots of different types of star.

 Red dwarfs are smaller than our Sun. They burn fuel slowly, so they live a long time.

 Young solar systems Leftover material from a star's formation can turn into planets.

 Blue giants are among the hottest stars, and live for less than 100 million years.

 Supergiants are the rarest stars. They have short lives – under 50 million years.

291

A Universe is born

What was later termed the Big Bang was first proposed by Georges Lemaitre in 1931. Scientists believe it was the beginning of everything, but don't know what caused it to happen.

Georges Lemaitre

The Big Bang

Most scientists now believe that the Universe was born from a hot, dense spot more than 13 billion years ago. They call this event the Big Bang.

As the Universe expands and cools, at 300,000 years, matter as we know it starts to form. The Universe is a thousandth of its size today.

What happened?

Space and time were brought to life from a minute speck, which was unbelievably hot and heavy. The energy contained in this speck immediately began to spread out, in the form of an ever expanding fireball.

The Big Bang: "a day without yesterday."

Do you think the Big Bang was an explosion?

A long time coming

Matter only began to form hundreds of thousands of years after the Big Bang – long after the fireball had cooled. The resulting gases would form the stars, planets, and galaxies that exist today.

At 9 billion years the Universe looks much as it does today, if a little bit smaller. Our Sun starts to form.

Stars and galaxies start to form after about 300 million years.

What's that?

Scientists have detected a faint radio signal, present in any direction they look for it in space. They believe it is a faint glow from the Big Bang's superhot fireball. It is called The Cosmic Background Radiation.

The Cosmic Background Radiation was discovered by American physicists Arno Penzias and Robert Wilson in the 1960s.

No beginning, no end

An alternative to the Big Bang, the Steady State Theory claimed there was no beginning or end for the Universe. It's just always been there. Few scientists now believe in the Steady State Theory.

weird or what? The astronomer who gave the Big Bang theory its name didn't support it. He termed it Big Bang as a criticism and was surprised that the name stuck. He believed in the Steady State Theory.

No – it was more of an event.

Glossary

Acceleration Change of speed – speeding up or slowing down.

Alpine Areas on a mountain side that are above the trees but below the permanent snow.

Alveoli Tiny air sacs inside your lungs.

Amphibian An animal that can live on land or in water.

Ancestor Someone you are related to who lived a long time ago.

Astronaut A person who is trained to travel into space.

Astronomy The study of the universe.

Atmosphere The thin layer of gas that surrounds a planet.

Bacterium (plural: bacteria) A living thing with just one cell. Bacteria are found all over the world – in the oceans, on land, in plants, and in our bodies.

Carnivore An animal that eats meat. Lions are carnivores.

Cell A tiny unit that is the basic building block of all living things.

Chlorophyll The chemical in plants that makes them green. It is essential for photosynthesis.

Chromosome A rod-shaped strand containing DNA, found in the nucleus of a cell.

Civilization The way of life of a group of people living in a particular area – ancient Greek civilization, for example.

Condensation Changing from a less dense state, such as a gas, into a more solid state, such as a liquid – for example, water vapour condenses into water.

Continent A large area of land, usually divided into different countries. Europe is a continent.

Decibel The unit of measurement for sound.

Deciduous A plant that loses many or all its leaves in one season each year. Oak and maple trees are deciduous.

Decomposition The breaking down (decaying) of dead animals and plants into smaller pieces, and recycling them into nutrients.

Dermis The deepest layer of skin, which contains nerves and blood vessels.

Diaphragm The muscle under your lungs that moves up and down as you breathe.

Digestion The system that breaks down and absorbs food so your body can use it for energy and to make new cells.

DNA A chemical inside your body that contains the instructions for making living cells.

Ecosystem A community of plants and animals living and interacting with each other and their immediate environment.

Epidermis The top layer of skin, which you can see.

Equator The imaginary line around the middle of the world.

Era A period of time in history.

Estuary The place where a river meets the sea.

Evaporation The changing of a liquid to a gas.

Evergreen A plant that has leaves on it throughout the year.

Extinct An animal or plant that has completely disappeared from our world.

Fault A place where the Earth's crust has cracked and moved.

Fertilization The joining of a male cell and a female cell to start growing a baby OR improving soil by adding nutrients to it.

Fossil The remains of a plant or animal that has died and been preserved in rock.

Fossil fuels A fuel such as coal, oil, or natural gas that was formed underground millions of years ago from the remains of dead plants and animals.

Friction A force that makes things slow down. When two solids rub against each other, or when a solid moves through liquid or gas, it causes friction.

Galaxy A large rotating system of stars, gas, dust, and empty space held together by gravity.

Gene Part of your DNA, genes contain chemical information that controls the way your body develops and works. Genes pass from parents to their children.

Germ Tiny living thing (micro-organisms) found everywhere including inside our bodies. Bacteria are germs. Some germs are good, but some are bad and make us ill.

Geyser A naturally occurring hot spring, where occasionally the water boils and shoots up in a big spurt.

Glacier A huge river of ice.

Gladiator In Roman times, a man trained to fight other men or wild animals in an arena while others watched.

Gravity The attraction between everything in the universe. Gravity makes the moon rotate around the Earth, and the Earth and other planets rotate around the Sun.

Habitat The natural home of an animal or plant.

Herbivore An animal that eats mainly plants. Giraffes are herbivores.

Hibernation When animals rest through the winter. They normally find somewhere warm and dry and sleep throughout the cold season.

Hieroglyphics An ancient Egyptian method of writing that uses symbols.

Hydrosphere All the water on the Earth's surface, including ice, and water vapour in the atmosphere.

Immune system The cells and tissues in your body that protect it from infection. If you do get an illness, your immune system often creates special defences so you don't get the same illness again.

Inertia The tendency everything has to avoid movement or change.

Infrared radiation Heat energy that is given off by all solids, liquids, and gases.

Insulator Something that does not let heat or electricity travel through it very easily.

Invertebrate An animal without a backbone.

Irrigation Bringing water to land so plants can grow.

Mammal A warm-blooded animal that has fur and feeds its young with its own milk.

Mantle A layer of hot, solid rock that lies beneath the Earth's crust and surrounds the Earth's core.

Marsupial A mammal group in which the female has a pouch for its young.

Melanin A substance that our body produces to protect our skin from the sun.

Microchip A tiny electronic device used in computers and machines.

Mineral A solid with a crystal structure that is found in the ground

Monsoon A heavy rain-and-wind storm that occurs in southern Asia.

Morse code A system for sending messages using dashes and dots.

Mucus A sticky substance inside your airways that traps germs.

Mummy A dead body that has been preserved by removing some of the organs, treating the body with special chemicals, then wrapping it in long strips of cloth.

Nucleus Structure inside a cell that contains chromosomes and is essential for making proteins.

Nutrient A substance taken in by a plant or animal that is essential for its growth.

Nymphs Insects that have not yet become adults.

Omnivore An animal that eats both plants and meat.

Orbit The path that one object makes around another in space, while under the influence of gravity.

Ore A mineral that contains a metal.

Ornithischian Bird-hipped dinosaur.

Outback The remote, inland areas of Australia.

Pasteurization A process that uses heat to destroy bacteria in food.

Percussion A type of musical instrument that is hit or shaken to produce a sound.

Pharaoh A powerful ruler of ancient Egypt.

Photosynthesis The process by which plants use sunlight to make food from water and carbon dioxide in the air.

Planet A large, round object that orbits a star.

Population All the people or animals living in an area or country.

Predator An animal that kills other animals for food.

Reef A ridge of coral or rock just above or below the sea's surface.

Reflex action An automatic movement of your body that you can't control.

Religion The belief in, and worship of, a God or gods; a set of beliefs and way of doing things.

Reproduction The process by which animals and plants produce young.

Reptile A cold-blooded animal that usually lays eggs. Reptiles have tough, scaly skin.

Reservoir A man-made or natural lake where water is stored for use.

Runes Viking symbols used for writing.

Samurai An ancient Japanese warrior.

Saurischian Lizard-hipped dinosaur.

Savanna Tropical grassland with a few trees, found in east Africa and northern South America.

Scavenger An animal that rarely kills for food, but eats animals that have already died or been killed.

Space The large, almost empty, places beyond the Earth's atmosphere.

Spectator A person who watches an event.

Synthetic Made from man-made materials.

Transpiration The release of water vapour from a plant through small holes in the leaves.

Transplant When an organ is removed from someone's body because it is not working very well, and a new one is put in its place.

Tropical The area of land and sea on either side of the Equator.

Universe Everything! The Earth, moon, Sun, all the planets and all the galaxies – even those we haven't discovered yet.

Vaccination An injection that contains a very weak form of the virus or bacterium that you are being vaccinated against.

Vertebrate An animal with a backbone.

Virus A very tiny infectious agent that contains DNA and grows on living cells. Viruses cause disease in plants and animals.

X-ray A photograph that shows the inside of your body.

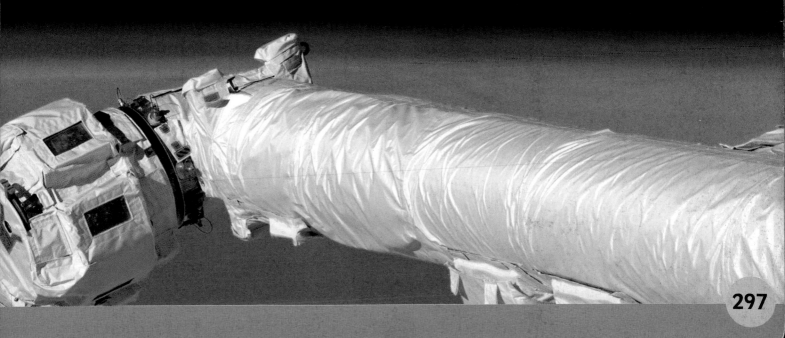

Index

Picture credits

The publisher would like to thank the following for their kind permission to reproduce their photographs:
(Key: a-above; b-below/bottom; c-centre; f-far; l-left; r-right; t-top)

Action Plus: Glyn Kirk 54crb (rugby player); **Aerofilms Ltd:** 89fcrb; **akg-images:** 93tl; **Alamy Images:** Ablestock 105bl; Arco Images GmbH/Thielmann, G. 259tc; Blickwinkel/Baesemann 155fcra; Bryan & Cherry Alexander Photography 55r; Andrew Butterton 267bl; Rosemary Calvert/ImageState 41fcra; Scott Camazine 125fcr, 264c; Nigel Cattlin 149cla; Croftsphoto 257tc; Phoebe Dunn/Stock Connection Distribution 112cra; eye35.com 239bl; Clynt Garnham 235br; Axel Hess 234b; Marc Hill 253tr; Esa Hiltula 20ftr (sauna); D. Hurst 125br; Images of Africa Photobank/David Keith Jones 255tc; ImageState/Pictor 105tc; ImageState/Pictor International 147r, 256bl; Janine Wiedel Photolibrary 101fc; Jeff Morgan Tourism and Leisure 196b; Jon Arnold Images Ltd 37cla; JupiterImages/Comstock Images 105cr (toilet); JupiterImages/Goodshoot 101tr; K-Photos 123c; Paul Andrew Lawrence 265fcr; Oleksiy Maksymenko 225ftr; The Natural History Museum, London 153bc, 153fbr; Ron Niebrugge 262tr; Edward Parker 260br; Andrew Paterson 232crb; Phototake Inc./Peter Treiber 257c; Rolf Richardson 36br; Robert Harding Picture Library Ltd/Ken Gillham 36clb; RubberBall Productions 104r, 105c, 105cra (boy), 105cr; Friedrich Saurer 125tl; Andy Selinger 155cb; Stock Connection Blue/Tom Brakefield 130-131; Stockfolio 555 217bl; 229br; Jerome Tisne (RF)/JupiterImages/Pixland 113tl; Visual&Written SL/Mark Conlin/VWPics 252cb; WoodySystem/McPhoto 252-253;**Ardea:** Piers Cavendish 14cra; Francois Gohier 190br; Stefan Meyers 176bl; Edwin Mickleburgh 57fbr; Pat Morris 139cr; Valerie Taylor 155fcr, 180clb; Zdenek Tunka 177cb, 177fcla; M. Watson 13clb; **ArenaPAL:** Fritz Curzon 72cb; **Atlantide Photo Travel:** 88cca; **Auto Express:** 35clb; **Bryan & Cherry Alexander Photography:** 10bl, 41ca, 159cr; RV0012-13 41fcla; 245crb; 49fcr, 270bl, 273br, 281br, 281ca; Noques Alain/Sygma 26fbr; Alan Schein Photography 43fcr; Paul Almasy 10crb (logs), 11tr (logs), 19ftl (boat), 38cr, 41fcl, 47ca; James L. Amos 9ftr; Roger Antrobus 87c; Archivo Iconografico, SA 27c, 82cla; Tony Arruza 12fclb, 23c; Yann Arthus-Bertrand 43clb; Craig Aurness 43fbr; Hinrich Baesemann/EPA 288cc; Roger Ball 29clb; Anthony Bannister/Gallo Images 141r; Dave Bartruff 50bc; Tom Bean 14cla; Annebicque Bernard/Sygma 26tr; Bettmann 22b, 56cb, 56fbl, 97tc, 279cb, 281clb, 283fcra; Bettmann/Francis G. Mayer 26fcrb; Bettmann/Neil Armstrong 280, 280c; Stefano Bianchetti 214cl; Christophe Boisvieux 21c; Georgina Bowater 45c; Michael Boys 254cl; Tom Brakefield 15bc, 15fbr, 27fbl; Andrew Brown/Ecoscene 253tc; Jan Butchofsky-Houser 37fcra; Car Culture 267tc; Philippe Caron/Sygma 23fbr; Michelle Chaplow 37clb; L. Clarke 53cb; Lloyd Cluff 248-249; Dean Conger 46fcra, 47fcla; W. Perry Conway 131tl; Richard Cummins 23cra; Barry Davies/Eye Ubiquitous 54cr; James Davis/Eye Ubiquitous 39cb, 81fcr, 86cra; Tim Davis/Davis Lynn Wildlife 56cla, 57ca; Michael DeYoung 158ca, 177ca; Carlos Dominguez 20bc; Laura Doss 100; Robert Dowling 28cr; EPA 263tl; Ric Ergenbright 40fbr; Douglas Faulkner 132-133c; Sandy Felsenthal 14cr; Ales Fevzer 76l; David Forman/Eye Ubiquitous 10cra (drill), 11tr (drill), 13fclb, 13fclb (drill), 43bc, 44tl; Owen Franken 47fclb (house); D. Robert & Lorri Franz 129r; Free Agents Limited/Dallas and John Heaton 29c, 34bc, 35cla, 48bl; Michael Freeman 38ftr, 44fcra, 50c; Fukuhara, Inc./Richard Fukuhara 51fcla; Paul Funston/Gallo Images 140cl; Jose Fuste Raga 28bc, 34clb; Colin Garratt/Milepost 92 ½ 23tr, 27tl; Raymond Gehman 10-11b; Todd Gipstein 32ca; Philippe Giraud/Sygma 18-19t; Darrell Gulin 14c (pelican); Dan Guravich 40fcra; Martin Harvey 131br; Jason Hawkes 23cr; Lindsay Hebberd 73cl; Chris Hellier 42b, 43ftl; John Holmes/Frank Lane Picture Agency 46crb, 47fcla (flower); Jeremy Horner 144ftr, 48fcrb; Scott Houston/Sygma 51tl; Carol Hughes/Gallo Images 140-141b; Peter Johnson 54cfbr (albatross), 168l, 169cla (crane); Jose Luis Pelaez, Inc. 101clb; Ray Juno 29cr; Wolfgang Kaehler 28fcrb, 41cb, 54crb (birds), 57cb; Steve Kaufman 12fcrb (bird), 50ca; Layne Kennedy 199tl; Thom Lang 104cl (brain); Maurizio Lanini 29cra; Alain Le Garsmeur 49cca; Danny Lehman 42ftr; Charles & Josette Lenars 47br, 89bl; Liu Liqun 49cl; Massimo Listri 28fcra; Yang Liu 49br; Craig Lovell 34br, 35bc, 51cl (train); Christophe Loviny 46cra; Renee Lynn 41crb; William Manning 13fcla; Dennis Marsico 55fbl; Jim McDonald 37bl; Joe McDonald 129bc; Sally A. Morgan/Ecoscene 27tc; Warren Morgan 54tr; Christopher J. Morris 31cl; David Muench 170c; Francesc Muntada 34tc; NASA 272ftr; NASA/EPA 283fcra (ss discovery); NASA/Roger Ressmeyer 272clb; Anthony Nex 19cra (house); Michael Nicholson 37c; Richard T. Nowitz 182-183; Diego Lezama Orezzoli 16fcra; Photo B. D. V. 75tl; Michael Pole 54fcr; Rick Price 57cla; Louie Psihoyos 185br, 190cl, 190cr, 191cr, 192-193b, 199tr, 202-203, 207t; Louie Psihoyos/Science Faction 190l, 191ftl, 201bl; Carl & Ann Purcell 38crb; Steve Raymer 36crb; Carmen Redondo 18cb, 35ftl; Roger Ressmeyer 23ca, 40cb; Reuter Raymond/Sygma 25c; Reuters/Sue Ogrocki 199br; Arthur Rothstein 38clb; Charles E. Rotkin 256cl; Galen Rowell 15fcra, 16br, 57cl, 57clb, 57fcl, 129cr; Erik Schaffer/Ecoscene 96-97c; Shepard Sherbell/Saba 57fcra; Paul A. Souders 21bl (sculpture), 52cb, 55fcl, 135cr, 164-165; David Stoeckin 29tr; Vince Streano 32tc; Keren Su 46cca, 48cla, 49tc; Paul J. Sutton/Duomo 221c; Sygma 253ftl; Liba Taylor 35cl; Roger Tidman 18crb, 56cra; David Turnley 41bcl; Peter Turnley 28cla, 43ca, 97bc; Van Parys/Sygma 25fcla; Vanni Archive 39cr; Brian A. Vikander 49fcl; Uwe Walz 28ca; Kennan Ward 159tr; Patrick Ward 23fcla (blackpool tower), 54l (background); Karl Weatherly 29cr; Chad Weckler 165tr; Robert Weight/Ecoscene 56-57tc; K.M. Westermann 18cb; Nik Wheeler 26ftr, 43cla, 43tl; Adam Woolfitt 29tl; Michael S. Yamashita 46fcr, 73tl; Jim Zuckerman 26bl, 193tr; **Dorling Kindersley:** The American Museum of Natural History 189cla (hypacrosaurus), 189clb (lambeosaurus), 197br; Bedrock Studios 182bc (plateosaurus); Board of Trustees of the Royal Armouries 81fcr (armour) 95tr, 95tr; Robert L. Braun - modelmaker 182tr (stegosaurus), 187ar (dilophosaurus), 187cb (stegosaurus), 197clb (styracosaurus); The British Library 60cb (books), 66fcla; The British Museum 44fcr, 81bl, 81fcrb, 83cra, 84bl, 84l, 85ca, 85cra, 87cra (book), 89tl, 93cr, 93cra; Centaur Studios – modelmakers 188tr; John Chase/The Museum of London 66bc, 66cra; Conaculta-Inah-Mex/Instituto Nacional De Antropologia E Historia 14fcr, 15fclb (stone head), 92fbr; Philip Dowell 16cr; Egyptian Museum, Cairo 80tr; Franklin Park Zoo, Boston 128cca;

Hasbro International Inc. 77tr; Jonathan Hateley – modelmaker 210r, 211fclb; Graham High at Centaur Studios - modelmaker 182br (brachiosaurus), 183bl (t-rex), 208cra (triceratops); Historiches Museum Der Stadt Wiend, Vienna 71ftl (programme); Jon Hughes/Bedrock Studios 1cl, 183fbl (gigantosaurus), 200cl; Imperial War Museum, London 217ftl; Index Stock/Alamy 240cb; Michael Jackson 25clb, 29cl (beer); Marwell Zoological Park, Winchester 20cr; Mattel Toys 77c; Judith Miller/Elms Lesters 121ftl; Museo Archeologico Nazionale di Napoli 33cla; Museum of the Order of St John, London 94clb; NASA 81c, 213r, 242cr, 271bl, 289tc; National Maritime Museum, London 49fcerb; National Trust 22fcrb; Natural History Museum, London 16cb, 46fcr, 49crb, 51el (oyster), 53fcl (opals), 82fcl, 82ftl, 134bl (tail/body feather), 134clb (inner wing), 134clb (outer wing), 134l, 135fclb (crow foot), 162ca, 185c, 185fcr, 189cla (parasaurolophus), 211cla (blue feather), 222br, 226tl, 231cr, 251fbr; The Natural History Museum, London 14ca; Odds Farm Park, High Wycombe, Bucks 22cr; Peabody Museum of Natural History, Yale University 202bl, 203tl; Pitt Rivers Museum, University of Oxford 71fcla (panpipes), 82br, 82cb; Powell-Cotton Museum, Kent 63cl; Luis Rey – modelmaker 183fbl (velociraptor), 202cla, 202ftl; Rough Guides 156cb (river), 185tr; Royal British Columbia Museum, Victoria, Canada 37br, 37clb, 81cra, 83cb; Saint Bride Printing Library, London 67cla; The Science Museum, London 2bl, 226c, 226cr, 226fcr; Senckenberg Nature Museum, Frankfurt 210bl; Neil Setchfield 12cb (hollywood); St Mungo, Glasgow Museums 63fcr, 65c; Statens Historiska Museum, Stockholm 91fcr; Stephen Oliver 66c, 67bc; University College, London 128fcla; University Museum of Archaeology and Anthropology, Cambridge 93cra (armlets); Wallace Collection 95cla; Barrie Watts 22cla (grass); Weymouth Sea Life Centre 21bc, 52fbl (octopus); Paul Wilkinson 217c; Jerry Young 8fcrb, 9c, 15fcl, 38tl, 41cl, 52cra (dingo), 156bl, 184c; **E & E Picture Library:** R. Nathwani 65tr; **ESA:** 271crb, 277fcr (satellite); **Financial Times:** 67cl, 67tr; **FLPA:** Flip De Nooyer/FN/Minden 211ftr, 211tr; Silvestris Fotoservice 162bl; D. P. Wilson 155fcrb; Konrad Wothe/Minden Pictures 173cr, 241b; **Getty Images:** 36cb (bobsleigh), 42cla; AFP 21tr; Altrendo Travel 68ca; Amana Images/Yoshio Otsuka 165br; The Bridgeman Art Library/German School 214c; James Burke/Time Life Pictures 249tr; David Cannon 17fcla; Cousteau Society 145cb; Adrian Dennis/AFP 23fcla; Discovery Channel Images/Jeff Foott 250-251; Robert Frerck 14tl; Gallo Images/Daryl Balfour 164cr; Iconica/Frank Whitney 239; The Image Bank/Alvis Upitis 20ftr (paper mill); The Image Bank/Antonio M. Rosario 272cr; The Image Bank/Antony Edwards 22fcra (angel); The Image Bank/Doug Allan 257cla; The Image Bank/Flip Chalfant 13c (seers tower); The Image Bank/Frans Lemmens 19c; The Image Bank/Jeremy Woodhouse 25r; The Image Bank/LWA 269ftr, 273cla; The Image Bank/Philippe Bourseiller 252cla; The Image Bank/Thomas Schmitt 52c (truck); The Image Bank/Tyler Stableford 243tr; David Kjaer 11fcr; National Geographic/Joel Sartore 233c; National Geographic/Klaus Nigge 200-201 (background); National Geographic/Michael K. Nichols 172bl; National Geographic/Michael S. Quinton 179crb; Panoramic Images 169fcla (stork); Photodisc 172cb (deciduous); Photodisc/David De Lossy 172c (conifer); Photodisc/Michael Goldman 86crb; Photographer's Choice/Georgette Douwma 122bl; Photographer's Choice/Marco Simoni 252fclb (headland); Redferns/Nicky J. Sims 71cb; Riser/Edwin Remsberg 13fcl; Riser/Georgette Douwma 145r; Riser/John R. Ramey 21bl; Riser/Philip and Karen Smith 248bc; Riser/Sightseeing Archive 280br; Riser/Terje Rakke 21fclb; Robert Harding World Imagery/Chris Rennie 37crb; Guido Alberto Rossi 32cr; Erik Simonsen 221tr; Stone/AEF - Yves Debay 19c; Stone/Anthony Cassidy 53clb; Stone/Art Wolfe 33clb (etna), 33cr (etna); Stone/Brett Baunton 35tr; Stone/Daryl Balfour 19ftl (mountain); Stone/David Sutherland 45r; Stone/Demetrio Carrasco 261tl; Stone/Frans Lemmens 24cla; Stone/Herb Schmitz 54bl; Stone/Hideo Kurihara 55fcla (geyser); Stone/Janet Gill 23tc (big ben); Stone/Joe Cornish 26cra; Stone/John Chard 170-171, 294-295; Stone/Joseph Devenney 15ca; Stone/Keith Wood 256-257; Stone/Ken Fisher 16c; Stone/Martin Puddy 45r; Stone/Michael Kelley 177tl; Stone/Paul Harris 88c; Stone/Pete Turner 12fcra; Stone/Siegfried Eigstler 166-167; Stone/Stephen Frink 13fbr; Stone/Steven Hunt 180tl; Stone/Tim Flach 111cla; Stone/Will & Deni McIntyre 15fcr; Stephen Studd/Photographer's Choice 160cra; Taxi 31cra; Taxi/Brian Kenney 189fclb; Taxi/Doug Corrance 22fcra; Taxi/Gary Bell 160l; Taxi/Getty Images 12fcrb, 16fcrb; Taxi/Jon Arnold 23cra (royal pavillion); Taxi/Michael Freeman 15cl (pyramid); Taxi/Peter Adams 44fcrb; Taxi/Steven Tax 51fcl (mt fuji); The Image Bank/Jeff Rotman 180-181; V. C. L. 93b; Heinrich Van Den Berg 127ca; Zhongda Zhang/IVPP 199c; **Tory Gordon-Harris:** 92cb, 92l; **Reproduced by permission of the Henry Moore Foundation:** 68cca; **Simon Holland:** Simon Holland and Victoria Waddington 73bc; **Hutchison Library:** Andrew Eames 40cra, 56fcrb; Robert Francis 94fcla (japanese castle); Isabella Tree 9cb (banks); **Images of Africa Photobank:** David Keith Jones 191b; **Imagestate:** Kord.com/Age Fotostock 51fcr; Pictor 15c (flamingos), 33fcl, 44cr, 47cra, 51fbl, 52fcr, 113bl; Pictor/Douglas David Seifert 14fcl; Pictor/Pfeil Davies 45fclb; Pictor/Randa Bishop 51fcl (geishas); **iStockphoto.com:** Kelly Cline 226bl; Esemelwe 235crb; Mark Evans 231tr; Filonmar 231br; Sergey Galushko 236crb (iron); Péter Gudella 239clb; Michaelangeloboy 227cl; NSPImages 238br (torch); Jurga R 235cra; Stephen Strathdee 147tr; Sylvanworks 233clb; **Morten Jensen:** 69cb; **Dr Marcus Junkelmann:** 88bl; **Kokoro Dinosaurs:** 211br; **Lebrecht Music and Arts:** Odile Noel 70l (b/ground); **Courtesy of Lockheed Martin Aeronautics Company, Palmdale:** 241t; **Lonely Planet Images:** Rhonda Gutenberg 38cra; Craig Pershouse 36br (crosses), 36tc; Tony Wheeler 39c; **NASA:** cl, cra, crb, 268b, 268fcl, 268fcl (sun), 268fcrb (astronaut), 269clb, 270-271 (b/ground), 276ca, 277ftr (shuttle), 277l, 278tl, 282, 282cfb, 283br, 283cl, 283tl, 284tr, 284-285, 285bc, 285cr, 285tr, 286cr (mqs), 286cr (viking), 286crb (mpl), 286crb (sojourner), 286tl, 286-287 (b/ground), 287br, 287cla, 287tr, 287tr, 288tbl (soho), 288fbl (trace), 288fclb (ulysses), 291br, 291cb, 296-297; ESA, H. Weaver (JHU/APL), A. Stern (SwRI), and the HST Pluto Companion Search Team 291tr; Finley Holiday Films 13crb; GRIN 97c; HQ-GRIN br; C. Mayhew & R. Simmon (NASA/GSFC), NOAA/NGDC, DMSP Digital Archive 6bl; MSFC br; **Natural Visions:** Richard Coomber 168cra; **The Natural History Museum, London:** 188cr, 189cl (brachylophosaurus), 191b; **naturepl.com:** Ingo Arndt 17br; Pete Cairns 179tc; Martin Dohrn 16-17cb; Georgette Douwma 145tl; Barry Mansell 175cla; Vincent Munier 50cla; T. J. Rich 41clb; Anup Shah 19r; Lynn M. Stone 44cl; **NHPA/Photoshot:** A.N.T. Photo Library 52fclb (snake), 131c; Laurie Campbell 136bl; Bill Coster 41ftl; Andrea Ferrari 194-195; Martin Harvey 168-169; Adrian Hepworth 162-163; Daniel Heuclin 130fcra

(tree-kangaroo), 138cra (caecilian), 139crb, 169tr; Hellio & Van Ingen 159br; Burt Jones & Maurine Shimlock 52fclb (snail); Gerard Lacz 133c; Andy Rouse 129fbl (dolphin); Jonathan & Angela Scott 129tl; Norbert Wu 133tr; **Nokia:** 97t (phone); **Photolibrary:** Don Farrall/White 265bl; Fresh Food Images/Amanda Heywood 40clb, 41fcrb; Gallo Images-Anthony Bannister/White 261cl; IFA Animals/IFA-Bilderteam GMBH 173tc; Paul Kay/OSF 146tr; Oxford Scientific (OSF)/Bert & Babs Wells 130fcra (numbat); Oxford Scientific (OSF)/David B Fleetham 52fclb (sea snake); Oxford Scientific (OSF)/Mike Powles 20cb; Oxford Scientific (OSF)/Roger Brown 130fcra (bandicoot); Oxford Scientific (OSF)/Thomas Haider 132l; Photodisc 226bc; Harold Taylor / OSF 155fbr; **Photoshot/World Pictures:** 20ca, 33br; Rudi Pigneter 46bl; **Pictorial Press Ltd:** 77crb; **Pictures Colour Library:** Charles Bowman 20br (geyser); George Hunter 10fbr (skyline); Edmund Nagele 23fbl; **Press Association Images:** Associated Press/John Rasmussen 90; Tony Marshall/Empics Sport 76tr; **PunchStock:** Digital Archive Japan 288ftl; **Robert Harding Picture Library:** 17fcl, 34tr, 44br, 75ca, 118c; Mohamed Amin 63ftr; Charles Bowman 24crb, 38tc; Jeremy Bright 62l; V. Englebert 92cr; Alain Evrard 60l; Robert Francis 93c; Miwako Ikeda/Int'l Stock 68-69b; D. Jacobs 53fcl; Roy Rainford 89cl; Luca Tettoni 64cra; Alison Wright 44bc; **Science Photo Library:** 103bc, 150fcr, 262-263, 292tl; Professors P. M. Motta, K. R. Porter & P. M. Andrews 115cla; Samuel Ashfield 152tr; Julian Baum 284cr; John Bavosi 108fclb; Biophoto Associates 114fcla; Tony Brain 121fcla; BSIP/Chassenet 239ftl, 239tl; BSIP/Dr T. Pichard 117cla; Dr. Jeremy Burgess 219tl; Chris Butler 290cl; China Great Wall Industry Corporation 276 (background); Costom Medical Stock Photo 114tc; Christian Darkin 118tr, 197tr; David A. Hardy, Futures: 50 Years In Space 274-275; Martin Dohrn 102fcra; John Durham 151tr; Bernhard Edmaier 8cl (background), 9cr (background), 209, 249tl; Eye Of Science 165cr; Vaughan Fleming 251bl; Mark Garlick 273tr, 290br, 290-291, 292-293; Adam Gault 153cl; Carlos Goldin 207tr; Steve Gschmeissner 103br, 103cl, 103fbl, 112cl, 116-117b, 148fcra; Adam Hart-Davis 287cr; Gary Hincks 262bl; JPL-CalTech/STSCI/VASSAR/NASA 269tl; Jerry Kinsman 213r; Ted Kinsman 215bl; Larry Landolfi 268c; G. Brad Lewis 225b; David Mack 152bl; J. L. Martra, Publiphoto Diffusion 104bl; Maximilian Stock Ltd 79crb; Astrid & Hanns-Frieder Michler 120clb (skin), 122cra; Mark Miller 153bl, 153br, 153cb, 153cl (background), 153cra, 153ftl, 153tl; Allan Morton/Dennis Milon 274cl; Prof. P. Motta/Dept. Of Anatomy/University "La Sapienza", Rome 114br; Dr. Gopal Murti 102br; NASA 78cr, 208-209b, 262bc, 283fcr (ss atlantis), 286clb; National Cancer Institute 110fcla; Dr. Yorgos Nikas 119tc, 119tl, 119tr; NREL/US Department Of Energy 224br; David Nunuk 269fcra; Laurie O'Keefe 192fclb; David Parker 198-199; David Parker For ESA/CNES/ArianeSpace 277crb; Physics Today Collection/American Institute of Physics 293cr; Alain Pol, ISM 115bc; Prof. Aaron Polliack 103bl; Detlev Van Ravenswaay 216fbr; Ria Novosti 276cb, 285cla; Paul Robbens & Gus York 279l; Royal Observatory, Edinburgh/AAO 269fcrb; Friedrich Saurer 280cra, 282bl, 284bl, 293bc; Francoise Sauze 238fclb; Karsten Schneider 263bc; Victor De Schwanberg 104fcl (heart), 104fcl (kidney); Science Source 151tl; SOHO/ESA/NASA 289; Andrew Syred 103cra, 112bc, 112crb; Sheila Terry 255fcla (loamy); US Geological Survey 216fbr; D. Van Ravenswaay 208clb; Detlev Van Ravenswaay 269fcr; Dr. Mark J. Winter 229cr; **Sean Hunter Photography:** 12cl, 31ftl, 32cr (pisa), 33clb (pisa); **Shutterstock:** Adisa 267c; Alle 126ftl; Andrei 215fcrb (family); Apollofoto 261br; Max Apps 252fbl (arch); Andrey Armyagov 217cra (car), 228bl; Orkhan Aslanov 221tl; Lara Barrett 124fbl (anemone); Giovanni Benintende 213c; Claudio Bertoloni 215fbr; Mircea Bezergheanu 264-2665; Murat Boylu 228bc; Melissa Brandes 250cb; Karel Brož 122br; Buquet 111clb; Michae Byrne 220b; William Casey 212fcr; CBPix 259c; Bonita R. Cheshier 230cr; Stephen Coburn 258-259b; Sahua D 242; Digitalite 212-213b; Pichugin Dmitry 124-125, 212clb, 224fclb (lake), 253cra, 258-259t; Denis Dryashk 151cr (pills); Neo Edmund 127fcrb (butterfly); Stasys Eidiejus 242tl; Elen 226-227 (background); Christopher Ewing 217cr (bulb); ExaMedia Photography 266tr; Martin Fischer 265r; Flashon Studio 232bl; Mark Gabrenya 148-149cb; Julien Grondin 213c; Jubal Harshaw 148br; Johan Hayman 154tr; Home Studio 230fbr, 231bc; Chris Howey 266l; Eric Isselée 126br; Jhaz Photography 235bl; Gail Johnson 155fttr; Kameel4u 237cdlb; Sebastian Kaulitzki 216cr; Nancy Kennedy 125fttr; Stephan Kerkhofs 156cb (reef); Tan Kian Khoon 111bl; Tamara Kulikova 265crb; Liga Lauzuma 154-155; Chris LeBoutillier 244cr; Francisco Amaral Leitão 257br; Luchschen 216crb; Robyn Mackenzie 233tl; Blazej Maksym 217cca; Hougaard Malan 148-149t; Patricia Marroquin 213clb; Martiii || Fluidworkshop 238ftl; Mashe 122fcr; Marek Mnich 233cca; Brett Mulcahy 235tl; Ted Nad 236cra; Karl Naundorf 234crb (pump); Cees Nooij 230l; Thomas Nord 221b; Aron Ingi Ólason 156bc; Oorka 266cfb; Orla 123tc; Pandapaw 126cl; Anita Patterson Peppers 238tr; Pcross 238bl; PhotoCreate 219cl; Jelena Popic 225ftl; Lee Prince 237cr; Nikita Rogul 224fbl (barbed wire); RPixs 244-245; Sandra Rugina 261br (dishwasher); Kirill Savellev 252fbl (stack); Elena Schweitzer 220c; Serp 147fcfr (maple); Elisei Shafer 259b (coral); Igor Smichkov 260l; Carolina K. Smith M.D. 228cl; Snowleopard1 123clb; Elena Solodovnikova 147cr, 147fbr (yellow ash); Ng Soo Jiun 147fbl; Specta 127bl; James Steidl 216tl; Teekaygee 124tl; Igor Terekhov 220cra; Tramper 254br; Ultimathule 229tc; Robert Paul Van Beets 216br; Vnlit 122fclb; Li Wa 216c; Linda Webb 214cra; R. T. Wohlstadter 263fcr; Jurgen Ziewe 214fbr, 258br; **Sony Computer Entertainment Europe:** 77tl; **Still Pictures:** 20fcrb; Biosphoto/Klein J.-L. & Hubert M.-L. 130c; John Cancalosi/Peter Arnold. Inc. 191tl; Sergio Hanquet 53r; Andreas Riedmiller 29crb; **SuperStock:** Age Fotostock 31bl, 218-219b; J. Beck 46cr; J. Silver 189b, 189r; Steve Vidler 51fcl (castle); **Warren Photographic:** 196t

All other images © Dorling Kindersley
For further information see: www.dkimages.com